IN-A-FLASH

PSAT

PSAT

Shirley Tarbell

Cathy Fillmore Hoyt

THOMSON

PETERSON'S

Australia • Canada • Mexico • Singapore • Spain • United Kingdom • United States

About Thomson Peterson's

Thomson Peterson's (www.petersons.com) is a leading provider of education information and advice, with books and online resources focusing on education search, test preparation, and financial aid. Its Web site offers searchable databases and interactive tools for contacting educational institutions, online practice tests and instruction, and planning tools for securing financial aid. Thomson Peterson's serves 110 million education consumers annually.

For more information, contact Thomson Peterson's,
2000 Lenox Drive, Lawrenceville, NJ 08648; 800-338-3282;
or find us on the World Wide Web at www.petersons.com/about.

Editor: Wallie Walker Hammond; Production Editor: Farah Pedley; Manufacturing Manager: Ray Golaszewski; Composition Manager: Gary Rozmierski; Cover Design: Allison Sullivan; Interior Design: Gary Rozmierski.

ISBN 0-7689-1416-7

Printed in Canada

10 9 8 7 6 5 4 3 2 1   06 05 04

Fifth Edition

CONTENTS

INTRODUCTION: LET'S GET ORGANIZED

About the Test (pages 2–5) describes the PSAT/NMSQT and answers some basic questions you may have. Be sure to spend a few minutes reading **How to Use This Book** (pages 6–8), which includes study plans for both the Questions, Strategies, and Exercises sections, as well as the practice test. After you review **Test-Taking Tips** on pages 9–11, you will be ready to begin studying for the test.

Don't worry. We're going to prepare you for the PSAT . . . in a flash!

ABOUT THE TEST

What Is the PSAT/NMSQT?

Welcome to the world of the Preliminary SAT/National Merit Scholarship Qualifying Test. The PSAT/NMSQT is a standardized test used to measure how well you can do college-level work. The test measures skills in

- Verbal reasoning
- Critical reading
- Mathematical problem solving
- Writing

It does not measure your knowledge of specific facts.

The PSAT/NMSQT is cosponsored by the College Board and the National Merit Scholarship Corporation. The Educational Testing Service (ETS) develops and administers the test (usually referred to simply as the Preliminary SAT or the PSAT). ETS also develops and administers the SAT. More than one million high school sophomores and juniors take the PSAT every year in October.

So, Why Should I Take the PSAT?

There are at least three good reasons for taking the PSAT:

1. The PSAT provides an opportunity to practice for the SAT I, which is a similar standardized test that you will likely take in your junior or senior year of high school. (Many colleges require you to take the SAT I and submit your scores when you apply for admission.) Colleges do not accept PSAT scores, so taking the PSAT really is a valuable chance to practice for the SAT I.

2. Registering for the PSAT enters you in several scholarship competitions, including the one for National Merit Scholarships. These scholarships can be used to help finance your college education.

3. Registering for the PSAT allows you to take advantage of the Student Search Service (SSS). The SSS matches students with prospective colleges. If you decide to participate in the SSS, colleges will mail you information that can help you select which schools to visit and apply to.

What Are National Merit Scholarships?

National Merit Scholarships are valuable financial awards given to outstanding college-bound students. The scholarship program is conducted by the National Merit Scholarship Corporation and is supported by grants from more than 600 corporations, colleges and universities, and other organizations. The top PSAT scorers in each state become semifinalists. Finalists, who must meet additional requirements, compete for one-time National Merit Scholarships worth $2,000 and for renewable four-year Merit Scholarships worth up to $8,000 per year.

Additional funds are available for promising African American high school students through the National Achievement Scholarship Program for Outstanding Black Students. Top scorers in each region compete for three types of Achievement Scholarship awards.

For more information about the National Merit Scholarship program, contact:

National Merit Scholarship Corporation
1560 Sherman Avenue, Suite 200
Evanston, IL 60201-4897
847-866-5100
www.nationalmerit.org

How Do I Register for the PSAT?

The PSAT is given every October at high schools across the United States. Registration is through your school; check with your guidance counselor about how to sign up. There is an $8.50 registration fee, although fee waivers may be available in certain situations. If your counselor does not have registration information, contact:

PSAT/NMSQT
P.O. Box 6720
Princeton, NJ 08541-6720
609-771-7070
www.collegeboard.org

How Is the PSAT Related to the SAT Tests?

The PSAT is a shorter, slightly easier version of the SAT I: Reasoning Test. You may have heard that the PSAT is changing. It will not be the PSAT that your brother, sister, or other relatives remember. In October 2004, a new PSAT will be administered for the first time. Both the PSAT and the SAT I contain the same types of multiple-choice questions that test critical reading and mathematical reasoning. Both tests include special math questions (student-produced responses) that require you to calculate answers. The writing skills section of the PSAT contains the same kinds of multiple-choice questions as the new SAT.

What Kinds of Questions Are on the PSAT?

There are several types of multiple-choice questions in the five sections of the test. Some types of questions, such as the sentence completion format, may be familiar to you from your school work. In the math section, there are also some problems, called student-produced responses, that require you to calculate answers on your own and then enter your answers on special answer grids. Each question type is described in detail in the Questions, Strategies, and Exercises sections of this book. The test is organized into five sections, as shown in the table below. Knowing what types of questions will appear on the test and how to approach each kind will help you do well on the test.

PSAT/NMSQT FORMAT

Section	Number of Questions	Time Limit (Minutes)
1. Critical Reading • Sentence Completion • Reading Skills—passages of 500–800 words • Reading Skills—short paragraphs of 100 words	24	25
2. Mathematics • Multiple Choice	19	25
3. Critical Reading • Sentence Completion • Reading Skills	24	25
4. Mathematics • Student-Produced Responses	19	25
5. Writing Skills • Identifying Sentence Errors • Improving Sentences • Improving Paragraphs	39	30

How Is the PSAT Scored?

Your test score is based on how many questions you answer correctly within the allotted time; there is a slight deduction (a fraction of a point) for each question you answer incorrectly. It is important that you pace yourself to answer as many questions as possible. Even though there is a small deduction for wrong answers, it still makes sense to guess at the correct answer if you are able to eliminate two or more options as definitely incorrect.

What If I Don't Score Well on the PSAT?

Your scores are not seen by colleges or used for admission decisions. If you are disappointed by your score, analyze what you can do to improve your skills in areas where you are weak. If you are a sophomore, you may take the PSAT again when you are a junior. If you are a junior, you cannot take the PSAT again, but you can use the PSAT as a learning experience. Focus on identifying where you made mistakes and apply that knowledge to preparing for the SAT I.

What Is the Best Way to Get Ready for the PSAT?

The best way to prepare for the test is to do well in school and take a wide variety of courses. Aside from that, it is important to become familiar with the format of the test, practice answering the types of questions you will be expected to answer on the PSAT, become accustomed to the pace at which you need to work, and be prepared physically, mentally, and emotionally on the day of the test.

Set up a study routine for yourself. Decide how and when to study based on how you work best: Early or late in the day? In many short sessions or several long ones? Alone or with a partner? The important thing is to have a routine. Work at the same time every day, in the same place, and make sure to stick to your plan. Be sure to start your study routine several weeks before the test so you have plenty of time to absorb the information. The next section tells you how to use this book to prepare for the PSAT. It also outlines a straightforward study plan that will help you organize your time.

Good Luck!

HOW TO USE THIS BOOK

This book is easy to use and was designed with the most effective study strategies in mind. The sooner you begin to prepare for the PSAT, the better off you'll be when test time rolls around. Reviewing the material in this book slowly and carefully will be much more effective than skimming it quickly a few days before the test. You will learn more, remember more, and be calmer and more confident on the day of the test if you establish a study plan and begin your review early.

Questions, Strategies, and Exercises

We suggest you proceed through this book chronologically, reviewing the Questions, Strategies, and Exercises sections first before moving on to the practice test in the back of the book. There is a Questions, Strategies, and Exercises section for each main skill area on the PSAT: Critical Reading, Mathematics, and Writing Skills. The chapters are divided into units that describe and explain each type of question you will see on the test. Along the way you'll learn important strategies for answering each kind of question. The text also will help you understand why the correct answer is the best response and why the other options are incorrect.

As you become acquainted with each question type, you will have an opportunity to practice answering some sample questions in a short exercise at the end of the unit. Each exercise is followed by detailed answer explanations that help you understand which answer is best and why. Relevant strategies and tips are also included in the answer explanations.

You can work through the Questions, Strategies, and Exercises sections one unit at a time, focusing on one type of question in each session, as shown in the study plan on page 7. If you work better in longer study sessions, simply combine the sessions in the study plan into logical blocks of time.

Practice Test

Once you are familiar with the different types of questions and the strategies needed for answering them, you are ready to take a practice test. The practice test in this book is very similar to the actual PSAT in terms of content, format, types of questions, difficulty level, and length. Taking a practice test that is similar to the actual test is one of the best ways to prepare for the real test.

STUDY PLAN: QUESTIONS, STRATEGIES, AND EXERCISES

Session	Minutes	Section	Activities
1	25–45	Critical Reading	Read **Sentence Completion** unit Complete Exercise
2	25–45	Critical Reading	Read **Critical Reading** unit Complete Exercise
3	15–30	Critical Reading	Review problematic questions and answer explanations
4	25–45	Mathematics	Read **Multiple-Choice Questions** unit Complete Exercise
5	25–45	Mathematics	Read **Student-Produced Responses** unit Complete Exercise
6	15–30	Mathematics	Review problematic questions and answer explanations
7	25–45	Writing Skills	Read **Identifying Sentence Errors** unit Complete Exercise
8	25–45	Writing Skills	Read **Improving Sentences** unit Complete Exercise
9	25–45	Writing Skills	Read **Improving Paragraphs** unit Complete Exercise
10	15–30	Writing Skills	Review problematic questions and answer explanations
11	15	Test-Taking Tips	Review the test-taking tips on pp.9–11

The practice test in this book differs from the actual PSAT in one important way: Each page in the practice test contains no more than two questions, with the answers and explanations immediately following on the next page. This format gives you instant feedback on the answers you selected and immediately clarifies why the correct answer is the best response. This approach ensures that you understand the questions as you go along so that you maximize your study time and gain knowledge and experience with each question. Once you are thoroughly familiar with the kinds of questions on the test, you can take a full practice test under timed test conditions for the most accurate results.

When you take the practice test in this book, try to imitate the actual test as much as possible. Sit at a table or desk in a quiet room free of distractions and

STUDY PLAN: PRACTICE TEST

Session	Minutes	Activities
1	45–75	Answer questions and review answers in **Section 1:** Critical Reading
2	45–75	Answer questions and review answers in **Section 2:** Mathematics
3	45–75	Answer questions and review answers in **Section 3:** Critical Reading
4	45–75	Answer questions and review answers in **Section 4:** Mathematics
5	45–75	Answer questions and review answers in **Section 5:** Writing Skills
6	30–60	Review Questions, Strategies, and Exercises sections for question types you found difficult

work through one full section at a time. The actual test is 2 hours and 10 minutes, but you need not time yourself during the practice test in this book. Simply work through each section, answering two questions, then reviewing the answer explanations on the following page as you proceed. Working through an entire section at one sitting will give you a realistic idea of what the actual PSAT is like. Your study plan for the practice test might look like the one below.

Be sure to review all the answer explanations, even for the questions you got right. You want to be certain that you selected the correct response for the right reason. Notice any general weaknesses you have, and review those sections again in the Questions, Strategies, and Exercises sections. If you want to take another full-length practice test before the test date, check with your counselor for a copy of *The PSAT/NMSQT Student Bulletin*. This free publication includes a practice test, a score sheet, and directions for calculating your score.

TEST-TAKING TIPS

The best way to do well on the PSAT is to know what to expect on the day of the test. Here are some test-taking tips to help you do your best.

Be Familiar with the Format of the Test

Know how many sections there are, how much time is allotted for each, and what kinds of questions will be asked. Be aware that questions in each section are arranged by difficulty, with easy questions in the beginning and harder questions near the end. (Note that critical reading questions and the writing skills section on improving paragraphs are not arranged by difficulty.)

Understand the Directions for Each Question Type

Learn the directions for each type of question. The directions in this book are very similar to those on the actual test. Understanding the directions ahead of time will save you valuable time on the day of the test.

Complete Your Answer Sheet Carefully

Be sure to mark your answer sheet correctly by filling in answers on the correct line. Mark the ovals accurately and be sure to erase completely should you decide to change an answer. Be careful to avoid making stray marks on your answer sheet or your test may be mis-scored.

Pace Yourself

Wear a reliable watch. As you begin each section, figure out the ending time of that section according to your watch and write that time in your test booklet. It's important to always know how much time you have left. Don't spend too much time on any one question; skip difficult questions and return to them later if you have time.

Use your time wisely during breaks, too. Get a drink of water, use the restroom, stretch, relax, and clear your mind. Get mentally prepared for the next section by thinking ahead and visualizing doing well. Do not dwell on, or even think about, the sections that you have already taken.

Write in Your Test Booklet

You will not be given scrap paper, but you can write in your test booklet. When you begin a new section, record the time at which you need to stop working. As you work through the sections, cross out answers you've eliminated, underline or make notes in reading passages, and draw diagrams and write equations that help you solve math problems. No one will see what you write in your test booklet, so make any kind of marks or notations that help you work quickly and accurately.

Answer Easy Questions First

All questions—easy and difficult—are weighted equally. Because you get the same amount of credit for an easy question as a hard one, you might as well get points for questions you're most sure of. Answer the easy questions first, then return to the more difficult questions.

Use the Process of Elimination to Make an Educated Guess

If you're not sure which choice is right, try to eliminate choices that you know are wrong. Every choice you eliminate improves your odds of guessing correctly. Remember that your score is based on the number of questions you answer correctly, minus a small deduction for questions answered incorrectly. If you can eliminate two or more choices as clearly wrong, it may be worth it to make an educated guess.

Skip Difficult Questions

If you can't eliminate any choices, you're better off skipping the question. Don't waste time on questions that are too difficult for you. You can still achieve a high score even if you miss a few questions.

Review Answers to Each Section

If you finish before the time is up for a section, you may look over *that section* of the test. It is a good idea to check your answer sheet to be sure that you've answered all the questions on the right line. If you have a good reason for changing an answer, go ahead. But be careful about changing an answer unless you find a careless error. Usually your first answer is best.

Be Confident and Calm

Do your best with the knowledge that you are ready for this test. Even if you don't know an answer, stay calm and positive. Don't dwell on what's difficult or start doubting yourself. Some questions are *supposed* to be hard, and you're not the only person in the room who's struggling with the tough ones. The best way to meet the challenge is to take it one step at a time and keep a positive focus.

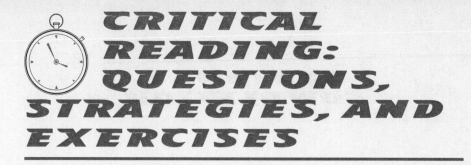

CRITICAL READING: QUESTIONS, STRATEGIES, AND EXERCISES

The Critical Reading portion of the PSAT measures your vocabulary, your ability to understand the logic of sentences and paragraphs, your ability to understand the relationship between words and concepts, and your ability to read and understand written material.

There are two main sections in the Critical Reading portion of the PSAT:

1. Sentence Completion

2. Critical Reading (includes short and long reading passages)

SENTENCE COMPLETION

Sentence completion questions will present you with a statement that contains either one or two blanks. You will then be asked to pick out, from five choices, the word (or words) that, when put into the blank, will *best* complete the meaning of the sentence as a whole. In some instances only one word will be missing; in other instances, two words will be missing.

Sentence completion questions test two main attributes:

- The strength of your vocabulary

- Your general verbal ability, especially your ability to understand the *logic* of sentences

To improve your vocabulary, you should *read* as widely as you can between now and the time of the test, looking up words you do not recognize. To improve your general verbal ability, you should *practice*, using the exercises in this book. If you do both these things, you will substantially improve your score on the PSAT.

Following are some examples of kinds of questions you will find in the practice test in this book and on the actual PSAT test, along with methods of finding the right answers. There are four main strategies for dealing with all types of sentences:

1. Read the sentence for its *overall meaning* and *internal logic*, then quickly look over the choices—many times, this strategy alone will point you toward the answer, since your common sense may tell you that two or three of the choices (or four, if you are lucky) do not fit at all.

2. *Eliminate* as many of the obvious wrong choices as you can.

3. Look at *key words* that may point you to the meaning, words that introduce the sentence or link its parts together—for example, *as, since, because, however, similarly, yet, therefore*, and many others.

4. When confronted with a complex sentence, *simplify* it as much as you can.

The three main types of sentences you will find on the PSAT are:

1. **Cause-and-effect** sentences—that is, what is said in one part of the sentence causes what is said in the other.

   Since he believed in ghosts himself, Myron found Susan's statement that she had seen a weird mist emanating from her bedroom mirror entirely _____.

   (A) plausible
   (B) outlandish
   (C) spontaneous
   (D) incredible
   (E) neutral

The correct answer is (A). Look at the overall meaning and simplify the sentence as much as possible: What are the facts?

   Myron believed in ghosts.
   Susan saw a weird mist coming from her mirror.

Now look for key words that might point to the kind of sentence this is. The word *since* indicates cause-and-effect. Now look at the choices to see which can be eliminated. The first choice looks good—a person who believes in ghosts would likely believe, or find *plausible*, a weird mist coming from a mirror. Certainly he wouldn't find it *outlandish* or *incredible*, so you can eliminate choices (B) and (D) right away. He might believe the mist to be *spontaneous,* and he might even feel *neutral* about it (although common sense says that this is doubtful), but these choices, (C) and (E), would not involve cause-and-effect. So choice (A), *plausible*, is the most logical answer. Of course, you have to know what that word means, which is where your habit of reading widely comes in!

2. **Comparison/contrast** sentences—that is, sentences that show ways in which two things are the same as, or different from, each other.

   Consciousness is the most obvious and _____ feature of the human mind; however, it is also the most _____.

   (A) devious . . . celebrated
   (B) humdrum . . . sensational
   (C) remarkable . . . miraculous
   (D) familiar . . . mysterious
   (E) puzzling . . . enigmatic

The correct answer is (D). Your common sense will tell you that consciousness by itself is neither *devious* nor *humdrum*, so choices (A) and (B) can be scratched at the beginning. Now look at the remaining three choices. Consciousness is *remarkable* and *familiar* to us all, and—if we think hard about it—consciousness is very *puzzling*. Now look at the important key word, *however.* This points to a contrast. Neither choice (C) nor choice (E) contains contrasting words—something that is *miraculous* is *remarkable*, and the words *puzzling* and *enigmatic* are very close in meaning. So we are left with choice (D), which does contain contrasting words, *familiar* and *mysterious.*

3. **Definition** sentences—that is, sentences in which one part defines another.

   Abraham is a fine athlete—tall, _____, and superbly fit.

   (A) articulate
   (B) ungainly
   (C) supercilious
   (D) morose
   (E) robust

The correct answer is (E). Even a cursory reading of this sentence indicates it contains a definition—the important key word here is the word *is.* Your own common sense, as well as your vocabulary, will tell you that a good athlete is not *ungainly,* nor is he necessarily *articulate, supercilious,* or *morose* (he may be all three, but these characteristics have nothing to do with the fact that he is an athlete). A good athlete is almost certainly *robust,* however, so the right answer is clearly choice (E).

EXERCISE

DIRECTIONS: Each of the following sentences has either one or two blanks, each representing a word or words needed to finish the sentence. Each sentence is followed by five words or sets of words marked (A) through (E). From these five choices, pick the one that best completes the meaning of the sentence as a whole. When you are finished, look at the answers to see how you did. If you missed some questions, the answer explanations will help you see where you went astray.

1. Because they tend to involve dramatic and wondrous happenings—and because they demand no _____ proof—the pronouncements of superstition are often more _____ than those of science.

    (A) disruptive . . . repugnant
    (B) troublesome . . . appealing
    (C) apparent . . . appalling
    (D) reliable . . . suspicious
    (E) difficult . . . tedious

2. When it became apparent that they could not _____, the rebels fled into the hills.

    (A) survey
    (B) prevail
    (C) convey
    (D) require
    (E) permit

3. Betsy never liked Norman, so none of us found it _____ that it might be she who had slipped the poison into his custard.

    (A) predictable
    (B) notorious
    (C) palatable
    (D) inconceivable
    (E) reprehensible

4. He is a wonderfully _____ musician, playing the zither and the bagpipes with equal aplomb.

    (A) sincere
    (B) harmonious
    (C) respectable
    (D) prosperous
    (E) versatile

5. The woman was a/an _____ speaker, who could _____ anyone of anything.

    (A) diverse . . . divest
    (B) admirable . . . deprive
    (C) morose . . . enjoin
    (D) devious . . . unburden
    (E) persuasive . . . convince

6. At first we believed the man to be _____, since he was able to _____, almost to the minute, when the next robbery would occur, enabling the police to catch the crooks.

    (A) psychic . . . predict
    (B) irrational . . . designate
    (C) deranged . . . foretell
    (D) fastidious . . . recount
    (E) ingenious . . . prevent

7. The girl always appeared cold and _____, so we were surprised that she showed so much affection for the new rottweiler puppy.

   (A) impressionable
   (B) insensitive
   (C) depressed
   (D) serene
   (E) obstinate

8. Formerly _____ as a "dumb blond," Marilyn Monroe is now _____ as having been an intelligent, sensitive woman.

   (A) sensationalized . . . romanticized
   (B) sabotaged . . . described
   (C) denigrated . . . lauded
   (D) recognized . . . remarked upon
   (E) romanticized . . . redeemed

ANSWERS AND EXPLANATIONS

1. **The correct answer is (B).** Immediately, the word *because* alerts you that this is a cause-and-effect sentence. You are next confronted by the words *dramatic and wondrous*, words that have generally positive meanings. Without reading further, go to the answer choices and look for positive words; the only one is the second word in choice (B), *appealing*. Now, to double-check, go back and simplify the sentence:

   Because dramatic and wondrous: appealing.

   You need not even regard the first blank—you've found the most logical answer. Read the sentence over, though, with both words in choice (B) inserted into the blanks, just to make sure. You'll find the statement does make logical sense.

2. **The correct answer is (B).** This is a cause-and-effect sentence, telling the reason the rebels fled into the hills. Here your own common sense is the best guide. What do *rebels* strive to do? Why, *prevail*, of course. They may *survey, convey, require*, or *permit*, but these descriptions are not intrinsic to being a rebel. So you need go no further—again, you have found the logical answer.

3. **The correct answer is (D).** The key here is the tiny word *so*, alerting you that this is a cause-and-effect sentence. Now look at the first part of the sentence:

   Betsy never liked Norman . . .

   What did this state of affairs cause? It caused us NOT to do something (that is, *none of us* did something). Now look at the sentence as a whole again, and analyze it using your common sense. Probably we would *all* find it *predictable, notorious*, and *reprehensible* for Betsy to slip poison into Norman's custard, so choices (A), (B), and (E) are ruled out. It is likely that *none of us* would find Betsy's actions *palatable*; however, this would have nothing to do with the fact that Betsy never liked Norman. Logically, then, only the word *inconceivable* completes the sentence as a whole.

4. **The correct answer is (E).** Using your common sense you can see that the second half of the sentence defines the first. (There is no key word indicating cause-and-effect or comparison/contrast; there is only the statement *He is* . . .) And what does his playing such disparate instruments as the zither and the bagpipes have to do with his being *sincere, harmonious, respectable*, or *prosperous*? Very little. Such playing would, however, point to his being *versatile*—so long, that is, as you know what the word means. Here your vocabulary, as well as your logic and common sense, is being tested.

5. **The correct answer is (E).** Here, again, is a definition sentence, with no words to indicate causation or comparison/contrast. So you can assume that the second word defines the first. To be *diverse* does not logically mean to *divest* anyone of anything—in fact, such a sentence would make no sense. The same is true of the other choices, until we get to the last one. To be *persuasive* means to be able to *convince* people. And so you have your answer.

6. **The correct answer is (A).** Note the key word *since*, pointing to this being a cause-and-effect sentence. Now simplify:

   > The man was (something), which caused him to be able to do (something else).

   > The man enables the police to catch crooks.

   It's not likely that an *irrational* or *deranged* person could help the police (at least that is not the most logical choice). Being *fastidious* would have nothing to do with having such powers. Being *ingenious* might fit, but *prevent* would not. (The statement "He was able to *prevent* . . . when the next robbery would occur" makes no sense.) So you are left with choice (A), which is the most logical choice, since what *psychics* mainly do is *predict*.

7. **The correct answer is (B).** There are two keys to the answer. First are the key words *and* and *so*. The girl was cold *and* (something), so we were surprised. This is therefore a cause-and-effect sentence. Would we be surprised that an *impressionable, depressed, serene,* or *obstinate* person showed affection? No, we would not necessarily be surprised. Would we be surprised that an *insensitive* person showed affection? Definitely. Moreover, the first part of the sentence makes sense—the words *cold* and *insensitive* logically belong together.

8. **The correct answer is (C).** Your logic will tell you immediately that the sentence is one of *contrast* ("*dumb blond*" and *intelligent, sensitive*; as well as *formerly* and *now*). Given the choices, only (C) contains contrasting words and therefore is the most logical answer.

CRITICAL READING

The critical reading section of the PSAT is one of the most important sections, since success in college depends directly on your ability to read and understand written material. Critical reading items will include reading passages that are approximately 100 words, followed by 1 to 3 questions, and 400 to 850 words long, followed by a number of questions. The critical reading section of the PSAT is designed to test your ability to do the following:

- Determine the meaning of a **word in context**. The meaning of a word depends on the words that surround it. For instance, the word *foot* means something very different in the following sentences:

  I hurt my *foot*.
  I can *foot* the bill.

- Understand **basic facts** stated in the passage—that is, those things the passage says are certainly true.

- Be able to pinpoint the **main idea** of the passage. Usually it is a generalization. Beware of choosing answers that are too narrow and specific.

- **Compare and contrast** two passages on the same subject or two ideas contained within the same passage.

- **Relate** parts of a passage to the whole passage or to other parts of it.

- **Analyze and evaluate** the passage in terms of its logic, implications, ideas, opinions, and arguments, including recognizing inconsistencies in arguments.

- Identify the **organizational techniques** used by the author.

- Identify the **author's intent** in writing the passage and **attitude** toward the subject.

To do well on the critical reading questions, you must

- Become **involved** in what you're reading

- Look for **key words** to help you find the meaning

- Remember that **the answers are in the passage**—you won't be asked for outside knowledge of the subject

Following is a 575-word passage, such as you may find on the PSAT. It is followed by five questions based on its content. Answer the questions based on what is *stated* or *implied* in the passage. Then read the answer explanation after each question to learn how to think through the critical reading questions.

This passage deals with bats, their characteristics, and our attitudes toward them.

Line The bat has long been a symbol of evil because of its nocturnal habits; its strange, hairless wings; and its face, which resembles the faces of gargoyles found on medieval cathedrals. Yet the bat is, in fact, not only a harmless creature but also a beneficial one—the vampire bat being the
5   single exception (found only in Latin America and preying mainly on cattle, which are not even awakened from sleep by the small bat bites) in the nearly thousand species that exist in all parts of the world.

Bats are helpful to our environment in many ways. According to Bat Conservation International, an organization devoted to saving endangered
10   species of bats, the forty species found in the United States consume enormous numbers of insect pests that plague American farmers—beetles, locusts, and leafhoppers. In fact, it is the main predator of nocturnal flying insects; one colony of insectivore bats can eat several tons of mosquitos in a single night. Fruit- and nectar-eating bats are a source of pollination for
15   night-blooming flowers and dispersal of seeds for fruit, such as bananas and mangoes, and for nearly 300 other plant species. In the world's tropics, bats are essential to the very existence of the rain forests. Even the much-maligned vampire bat (*Desmodus rotundus*) is beneficial to us. An anticoagulant found in its saliva was recently patented by Merck
20   Pharmaceutical Company for use as a blood thinner for heart patients.

Bats are found in all parts of the world except extreme desert and arctic regions. They come in a variety of shapes and sizes: their faces range from gargoyle-like to fox-like, their sizes from that of the tropical bat (actually called the "flying fox"), which has a wingspan of six feet, to the
25   "bumblebee bat," which weighs only ounces. Bats are not flying rodents; rather, they belong to the order Chiroptera and are more closely related to primates (including humans) than to the rat. Their arms and the bones of their hands resemble those of primates, and they have canine teeth rather than large incisors. They are not nearly as apt to spread rabies as are other
30   wild animals or even as unvaccinated domestic dogs and cats; the danger of becoming ill from contact with a bat is extremely remote. And because they navigate by echolocation (using the echos from their high-pitched squeaks to locate objects in their paths, even in total darkness) they will never—unless you enclose them in a small place and frighten them nearly
35   to death—run into you, let alone become entangled in your hair. They are the only mammal capable of true flight and have been on the earth for 50 million years, since the time of the dinosaur.

Yet few animals—in fact, the snake may be the only one—suffer more malicious persecution. The main exception is in China, where the
40   bat is seen as a symbol of good luck; in most other parts of the world it is viewed with superstition and fear. Bats feature prominently as figures of evil in Hollywood movies; they are a staple for scaring children at Halloween; thanks to Shakespeare, they are thought of as a main ingredient in witch's brew ("eye of newt, and . . ./Wool of bat"); and in
45   medieval drawings, their wings are often seen attached to the devil. Because of human imagination and groundless myths, these fragile, helpful creatures are in serious decline. Many species, in fact, face extinction, and if this occurs, it will be to the great detriment of fragile ecosystems all around the world.

1. Which of the following choices best represents the main idea of the passage?

   (A) In spite of their evil image, bats are not only harmless creatures but are also beneficial to humans.

   (B) Although bats are used to frighten children at Halloween, they are actually beneficial to humans in general.

   (C) Bats have been a symbol of evil throughout the ages, yet most species do no harm to humans at all.

   (D) Although most cultures detest bats, in China they are a symbol of good luck.

   (E) Bats have great variety, are able to fly by echolocation, and nurse their young.

The correct answer is (A). It is best, when faced with a "main idea" question, to first eliminate choices that are too broad and ones that are too narrow. Choices (B) and (D) are too narrow: Halloween and China are mentioned only once each—neither is a major part of the passage. Choice (C) is a little too narrow, leaving out the important idea that bats are beneficial to humankind. Choice (E) contains three details from the passage but doesn't sum the passage up. (Note the very specific detail "echolocation," mentioned only once in the passage.) Choice (A), however, is a generalization that encompasses three important ideas expressed in the passage—although bats have an evil image, they are not only harmless but also beneficial.

2. Based on the passage, which of the following best describes the author's attitude toward vampire bats?

   (A) The vampire bat is completely harmless, and all reports to the contrary are false.

   (B) The vampire bat is minimally harmful in one way, very helpful in another.

   (C) The vampire bat is the only extremely dangerous one out of the nearly thousand species of bat.

   (D) The vampire bat is the species most often used to scare children at Halloween.

   (E) The vampire bat is the one referred to in the line from Shakespeare quoted in the passage.

The correct answer is (B). Glance quickly at the passage and look at the details the author has selected to describe vampire bats. (They attack *mainly* cattle, and their bites are *small*. They are *much-maligned*, a near-cliché expression that means that their evil reputation is undeserved. Their saliva is used to treat heart patients.) Now, once again, eliminate the obvious wrong choices. Choices (A) and (C) can be scratched because they are refuted by these small details in the passage. Choices (D) and (E) are not found anywhere in the passage. Choice (B) fits.

3. Which of the following details about bats, not mentioned in the passage, would best support the author's main argument?

   (A) Fruit bats do not live in caves as most bats do, but roost upside down in trees.

   (B) Some bats have a life expectancy of around twenty years.

   (C) A few insects have evolved ways of protecting themselves from bats.

   (D) The bat uses echolocation to locate flying prey such as moths and mosquitos.

   (E) Bat guano (droppings) makes excellent fertilizer for organic gardening.

The correct answer is (E). The key word in the question is "argument." It implies that the correct answer will present some kind of value judgment. Choice (E) is the only choice that fulfills this requirement, supporting the author's argument that bats are *beneficial*. The other choices are simply nonjudgmental facts.

4. What is the main purpose of the mention of the structure of the bat's arms and hand-bones in paragraph 3?

(A) To demonstrate how interesting bat anatomy is

(B) To show that bats more closely resemble primates than rodents

(C) To demonstrate that bats are the only mammal capable of true flight

(D) To emphasize the bat's strange appearance, which is responsible for its poor image

(E) To show that bats are extremely well adapted to a wide variety of habitats

The correct answer is (B). First glance quickly at paragraph 3, especially at the sentences on either side of the detail in question. Eliminate the obvious wrong answers. Although the structure of the bat's arms and hands do have something to do with flight, choice (C), this fact is not mentioned in the passage. The detail does serve to make a bat's anatomy seem more interesting and does underscore the bat's strange appearance—choices (A) and (D)—but these points are not emphasized in paragraph 3. Choice (E) is implied in the passage but is irrelevant to the structure of the bat's arms and hands. Choice (B) follows directly after mention of the structure of the bat's arms and hands.

5. The author bolsters the main argument of the passage primarily by means of

(A) citing authoritative sources.

(B) appeal to our natural love of animals.

(C) analogies that compare bats with other creatures.

(D) concrete details about bats.

(E) citing scientific studies of bats.

The correct answer is (D). Regarding choice (A), the author cites only one authoritative source, Bat Conservation International. Although love of animals, choice (B), will help a person to be tolerant of the bat, this is not stressed in the passage. The passage contains only one analogy to another animal, choice (C), the snake. No scientific studies of bats are quoted, choice (E). There are many concrete details about bats in the passage, choice (D), so this is the right answer.

Here are shorter passages followed by one or two questions. Answer the questions based on what is *stated* or *implied* in the passage.

This passage is from the U.S. State Department Web site.

Line   In 1963, in Moscow, the Treaty Banning Nuclear Weapon Tests (. . .) was signed by the United States, Great Britain, and the Soviet Union. The Test Ban Treaty of 1963 prohibits nuclear weapons tests "or any other nuclear explosion" in the atmosphere, in outer space, and under water. While not
5   banning tests underground, the Treaty does prohibit nuclear explosions in this environment if they cause "radioactive debris to be present outside the territorial limits of the State under whose jurisdiction or control" the explosions were conducted. In accepting limitations on testing, the nuclear powers accepted as a common goal "an end to the contamination
10   of . . . [the human] environment by radioactive substances."

6. Which word best describes the Test Ban Treaty of 1963?
    (A) Comprehensive
    (B) Intensified
    (C) Inflated
    (D) Limited
    (E) Retroactive

The correct answer is (D). The treaty does not ban most underground testing. The other choices are not reflected in the passage.

7. The passage suggests that the main purpose of the treaty was to prevent global
    (A) warfare.
    (B) detonation.
    (C) pollution.
    (D) duplicity.
    (E) concession.

The correct answer is (C). The treaty states that a common goal is *an end to the contamination of . . . radioactive substances* in the human environment. Choice (B) is incorrect because the treaty allows for underground tests of nuclear weapons, suggesting that the prevention of detonations is not the main purpose of the treaty. The other choices are not supported by the passage.

This passage is based on an e-mail sent to Web site operators by the Federal Trade Commission beginning in November 2001.

Line   Your Web site claims that a product or therapy you sell is effective in the treatment or cure of anthrax, smallpox, or another disease or health hazard that may be associated with recent reports about threats of terrorism. We are aware of no scientific basis for such claims. Without
5   competent and reliable scientific evidence to substantiate these claims, the claims are illegal under the Federal Trade Commission Act and must be discontinued immediately. Violations of the FTC Act may result in legal action in the form of Federal District Court Injunction or Administrative Order. An order also may require that you pay money back to consumers.

8.   Which word best describes the purpose of the passage?

(A) Advice
(B) Warning
(C) Opinion
(D) Rejection
(E) Reminder

The correct answer is (B). The FTC e-mail threatens the Web site owner with legal action for noncompliance, so it is not merely *advice*, *opinion*, or *reminder*—choices (A), (C), or (E). Choice (D) does not make sense in the context of the passage.

9.   The main purpose of the FTC e-mail is to command Web site owners to

(A) repay consumers.
(B) cease making false claims.
(C) stop making terrorist threats.
(D) find scientific evidence for claims.
(E) inform consumers the claims are false.

The correct answer is (B). Choice (A) is wrong because the e-mail says only that *if* an order is issued, Web site owners *may* have to pay back money. Choice (D) is wrong because, although the e-mail says that *without . . . scientific evidence* owners must discontinue the claims, it does not order them to find it. Choices (C) and (E) are not supported by the passage.

This passage is adapted from an essay, "When Art and Morality Collide . . . ," by James Swafford (in National Endowment for the Arts magazine Humanities, July/August, 1997).

Line In the 19th century, writer Oscar Wilde produced works that were widely deemed immoral. Of that historical period, 20th century essayist James Swafford writes: What purpose do literature and the visual arts serve? What responsibilities must they assume? These were important questions
5 in the last century, as increasing literacy, inexpensive editions, the rise of lending libraries, public art exhibitions, and mass-produced prints from steel engravings made the verbal and visual arts available to the masses as never before . . . . Wilde ran afoul of [the expectation of moral purpose] on several occasions . . . . "All art is quite useless," announces the last line
10 of the preface to [Wilde's novel], *The Picture of Dorian Gray*.

10. According to Swafford, questions about the purpose of art were important in the last century, because art had become increasingly

   (A) admired.
   (B) accessible.
   (C) irresponsible.
   (D) anti-Evangelical.
   (E) nontraditional.

The correct answer is (B). The passage states that the questions became important when the arts became *available to the masses as never before* (lines 7–8). The other choices may be true but are not stated in the passage as a main reason.

11. What is the meaning of the phrase "ran afoul of" (line 8)?

   (A) Denied the existence of
   (B) Took up the cause of
   (C) Played a part in
   (D) Came in conflict with
   (E) Showed ignorance of

The correct answer is (D). The word *afoul* implies conflict. There is no evidence in the passage for the other choices.

EXERCISE

DIRECTIONS: The two passages below are followed by questions based on their content. Answer the questions based on what is *stated* or *implied* in each of the passages; some questions may also ask you to find a relationship between the passages. (The passages in the actual test will be longer; however, this will give you some idea of the kinds of questions you might be faced with.)

As noted previously, you might be given two passages that are related in some way. The passages might disagree about some subject or take differing perspectives on a single subject, or they might be about different subjects but have a similar perspective.

Both passages deal with the significance, or lack of significance, of dreams.

Passage 1

Line Every human society, from ancient times to modern times, has believed
    that dreams are deeply significant. Dreams have been said to enable us to
    have contact with deities and with the dead; they have been employed to
    foretell the future; and they are a main tool of modern psychology, dream
5   symbolism being used to delve into the most profound disturbances of the
    human mind. Sigmund Freud maintained that dreams are "the royal road to
    the subconscious mind."
        Although dreams are the result of electrical impulses in the brain
    during rapid-eye-movement (REM) sleep, they are much more than that.
10 That one can solve problems through dreams seems obvious to most
    people. Important scientific discoveries and artistic creations have begun
    in dreams. The discovery of the structure of the DNA molecule as a double
    helix was prompted by a dream of two snakes intertwined; the idea for the
    sewing machine came to inventor Elias Howe in a dream; and Robert
15 Lewis Stevenson is said to have had a dream that prompted the idea for his
    famous novel of good and evil, *Dr. Jekyll and Mr. Hyde*.
        A wide variety of people, artists and psychologists, scientists, and
    religious philosophers, believe that dreams have special significance—all
    believe that to ignore their power is to invite disaster.

Passage 2

20   Two Harvard researchers, Dr. Allan Hobson and Dr. Robert McCarley, have done research that would tend to debunk the idea that dreams have very much intrinsic significance. While admitting that it is possible for occasional meaningful symbolism to arise in sleep, these scientists believe that, in the main, dreams are the result of basic brain
25 processes rather than of spectral visits and other paranormal events or, as Freud thought, disguised fears and wishes.

      For Hobson and McCarley, the brain is a "dream state generator." Most dreams are simply the result of the human brain firing electrical impulses that arrive at the cortex during REM. The firings are random and,
30 in themselves, meaningless, these scientists say; dreams are merely a way in which the brain tries to make sense of the array of electrical signals that arrive at the cortex from the lower brainstem while we are sleeping. In dreams, Hobson and McCarley maintain, the brain is merely trying to construct a story to explain the input of disparate and unrelated data.

1. With which of the following statements would the author of Passage 1 and the scientists in Passage 2 likely NOT agree?

   (A) In dreams, the brain constructs stories.
   (B) Dreams occur during REM sleep.
   (C) Dreams are the result of electrical impulses in the brain.
   (D) The content of dreams should be thoughtfully attended to.
   (E) The process of dreaming is an area worthy of research.

2. The main point of Passage 1 is that

   (A) every human society, from ancient to modern times, has found significance in dreams.
   (B) dreams are an important tool of modern psychology, especially for delving into the subconscious mind.
   (C) although dreams arise from electrical impulses, they have deep significance beyond that.
   (D) dreams have given rise to important scientific discoveries and have inspired great literary works.
   (E) dreams occur during rapid-eye-movement sleep.

3. Hobson and McCarley would likely respond to the main argument of Passage 1 by saying that dreams are

   (A) only the products of overactive imaginations.
   (B) merely a physical process.
   (C) never symbolically meaningful.
   (D) simply phantasms constructed in the lower brainstem.
   (E) only occasionally the result of paranormal events.

4. The mention of intertwined snakes in paragraph 2 of Passage 1 is made mainly to demonstrate

   (A) the creative way in which the human brain makes important discoveries in dreams.

   (B) the way in which the human brain finds psychological significance in dreams.

   (C) the manner in which electrical impulses are transformed in dreams.

   (D) the way a DNA molecule is constructed.

   (E) Freud's idea of the "royal road to the subconscious mind."

5. With which of the following words would Hobson and McCarley most likely sum up the content of dreams?

   (A) Symbolic

   (B) Boring

   (C) Spectral

   (D) Delusional

   (E) Random

ANSWERS AND EXPLANATIONS

1. **The correct answer is (D).** The question is odd, since a quick reading of both passages would lead one to think that the author of Passage 1 and the two scientists in Passage 2 disagree about everything. One has to step back and consider what the main point of each passage is. The passages do not disagree about the causes of dreams, but rather about their *significance*. Then it becomes clear that the only choice of the five that deals with significance is choice (D).

2. **The correct answer is (C).** Approach this question by remembering that main points are usually generalizations. Choices that include only one or two specific details usually do not express a broad main point. None of the choices, except (C), is broad enough to be a main point—rather, they are details that support the main point.

3. **The correct answer is (B).** Hobson and McCarley's chief argument is that dreams are merely the physical process of random electrical firings in the brain. Choice (A) is incorrect because Passage 2 does not mention *overactive imaginations*. Choice (C) is incorrect because paragraph 1 admits that dreams contain occasional *meaningful symbolism*. Choice (D) is incorrect since paragraph 2 maintains that the electrical firings come from the lower brainstem, but the actual dreams are constructed after the firings arrive in the brain's cortex. Choice (E) is incorrect because it is directly contradicted in paragraph 1 of Passage 2.

4. **The correct answer is (A).** The only way to approach this question is to read paragraph 2 *carefully*, because all the choices are mentioned somewhere in the passage. The key word here is *discoveries*. Choices (B), (C), and (E) are not part of the discussion of discoveries. And the way a DNA molecule is constructed, choice (D), is only an incidental detail in the discussion of discoveries.

5. **The correct answer is (E).** Approach this question by asking yourself what the main point of the passage is and what the implications of the main point are. The entire final paragraph discusses the lack of meaning in dreams. The researchers imply that, since the firings that give rise to dreams are random and the data arriving at the brain are disparate and unrelated, the content of the dreams must be random, too. Choices (A) and (C) are contradicted in the passage. Choices (B) and (D) are not mentioned.

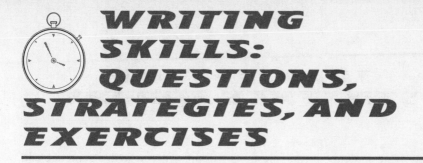

WRITING SKILLS: QUESTIONS, STRATEGIES, AND EXERCISES

The Writing Skills portion of the PSAT measures your ability to identify errors in usage and structure, to recognize sentences that are correctly written in standard English, and to make choices about improving the logic, coherence, and organization of faulty paragraphs.

There are three types of questions in the Writing Skills portion of the PSAT:

1. Identifying Sentence Errors

2. Improving Sentences

3. Improving Paragraphs

IDENTIFYING SENTENCE ERRORS

The identifying sentence errors questions will present you with a sentence and ask you to identify the mistake in it (there will be no more than one mistake, and in some cases there will be none). The error, if there is one, will be one of several underlined and lettered elements in the sentence. Elements of the sentence that are not underlined do not contain errors. In choosing answers, you must follow the rules of standard written English.

These questions are designed to test your knowledge of:

- Grammar

- Usage

- Word choice

- Idioms (a speech expression that means something beyond its individual words and cannot be translated exactly into another language—for example, "*many a day* has passed," or *according to* as opposed to the incorrect *according with*)

Here are some hints for answering identifying sentence errors questions:

- *Read the entire sentence first.*

- *Look at the underlined portions* to see if you can quickly spot an error.

- *If you see an error, mark your answer and move on* (remember, there will be only one error—if you spot it quickly, there's no need to linger).

- *If you don't see an error immediately, read the sentence again,* and if it sounds right to you, mark (E), *No error*, and move on.

The directions you'll find on the test will be similar to the following:

Directions: No sentence contains more than one error. The error, if there is one, is underlined and lettered; elements that are not underlined are correct. In choosing answers, follow the requirements of standard written English. If there is an error, select the <u>one underlined part</u> that must be changed to make the sentence correct, and fill in the corresponding oval on the answer sheet. If there is no error, fill in oval E.

Following are examples of identifying sentence errors questions that are similar to those on the PSAT.

That day, he knew he would have to wait in line; therefore, he will take
$\overline{}$ $\overline{}$ $\overline{}$
  A   **B**   **C**
a book along with him. No error.
         D   **E**

The correct answer is (C). There is a shift in tense from past (*he knew*) to future (*he will take*). The sentence should read: *That day, he knew he would have to wait in line; therefore, **he took** a book along.* Choice (A) is correct as an introductory phrase. The prepositions in choices (B) and (D) are used correctly.

Out my window, lurking behind some bushes, I saw a prowler and ran
  A   **B**   **C**
to the phone to call the police. No error.
       D   **E**

The correct answer is (B). The word order in the sentence is illogical. The phrase *lurking behind some bushes* is a misplaced modifier. In context, it is meant to describe *prowler*, not the speaker of the sentence who is presumably looking out the window. Choice (A) is a correctly written introductory phrase. Choice (C) is correct—*and ran*, is past tense, consistent with the verb *saw*. Choice (D) is a correctly written prepositional phrase. To correct the sentence, the modifier must be shifted to the right position: *Out my window, I saw a* ***prowler lurking behind some bushes*** *and ran to the phone to call the police.*

The principal told her that she must either comply to the rules of the
              A   **B**
school or face disciplinary action in the form of expulsion. No error.
  C   **D**   **E**

The correct answer is (B). The phrase *comply to* is the wrong form of the idiom *comply with*. When the correct idiom is used, the sentence reads: *The principal told her that she must either **comply with** the rules of the school or face disciplinary action in the form of expulsion.* Choice (A) consists of a logical verb and object; choice (C) is the correct form of the coordinating conjunction (*either . . . or*); and choice (D) is a correctly written prepositional phrase.

Marsha shouted loudly at Mabel as she was about to board the bus.
       A   **B**   **C**   **D**
No error.
  E

The correct answer is (C). The error is one of vague pronoun reference. The reader cannot tell whether it is Marsha or Mabel who is about to board the bus. A correct revision of the sentence might read: *As Marsha was about to board the bus, she shouted loudly at Mabel.* Choice (A) is a logical subject-verb agreement; choices (B) and (D) are logical prepositions with their objects.

I told <u>the people</u> gathered on the lawn that there was <u>someone</u> hiding
       A   **B**
<u>in the basement</u>, but <u>they didn't listen.</u> <u>No error.</u>
     C   **D**   **E**

The correct answer is (E). There are no errors in the sentence—it is written correctly in standard English.

EXERCISE

DIRECTIONS: No sentence contains more than one error. The error, if there is one, is underlined and lettered; elements that are not underlined are correct. In choosing answers, follow the requirements of standard written English. If there is an error, select the one underlined part that must be changed to make the sentence correct and fill in the corresponding oval on the answer sheet. If there is no error, select choice (E).

1. Both Janet and Tiffany want to be a veterinarian and work in zoos when
        A   B   C
    they grow up. No error.
        D   E

2. Antoine-Henri Becquerel, in 1896, a French physicist, discovered radioactivity
                         A   B
    when he exposed photographic film to uranium. No error.
            C   D   E

3. Fred's violin playing was better than Alice that evening, so Alice put away
                    A   B
    her instrument and left the grand concert hall. No error.
             C   D   E

4. To highlight a block of text such as a word, sentence, or paragraph, just
        A   B   C
    click and drag the mouse. No error.
        D   E

5. The three of them, Toni, Rajeev, and Manuel, goes sledding together
             A   B
    every weekend during the coldest part of the winter. No error.
        C   D   E

ANSWERS AND EXPLANATIONS

1. **The correct answer is (B).** Noun number agreement is faulty in this sentence. (Janet and Tiffany are two people; a veterinarian is one person.) Choice (A) is correct. *Both* is the correct modifier for two people. Choice (C) is correct because there is noun number agreement. Choice (D) is a correctly written object of the preposition *when*, and *they* is the correct pronoun to use for two people.

2. **The correct answer is (A).** The way the statement is written makes no sense, so begin by asking what happened in 1896. Logically, the discovery of radioactivity happened in 1896, so the phrase *in 1896* is a misplaced part that modifies *discovered radioactivity* and so belongs next to that phrase. Choice (B) is a correctly written past-tense verb and object; choice (C) is a correctly written noun and verb; and choice (D) is a correctly written prepositional phrase.

3. **The correct answer is (A).** The error is one of faulty comparison, and it's easy to miss. Presumably, Fred's violin playing was better than Alice's violin playing, not better than Alice herself. Be sure to read the sentence carefully, paying close attention to the underlined portion. Choice (B) is a correct coordinating conjunction. Choice (C) contains a correct coordinating conjunction and verb form. Choice (D) contains a noun with correct adjective forms.

4. **The correct answer is (E).** There are no errors in the sentence.

5. **The correct answer is (B).** This is faulty subject-verb agreement—the subject is plural, and the verb is singular. Choice (A) is a correctly written prepositional phrase. Choice (C) is a correctly written adjective and noun, as is choice (D).

IMPROVING SENTENCES

In the improving sentences portion of the PSAT, you will be presented with a number of sentences; part or all of each sentence will be underlined, and beneath each there will be five choices. The first choice will be to leave the sentence as it is; the other four choices will present ways to rephrase the underlined portion. Portions that are not underlined should remain the same. You will be asked to choose the most effective version of the sentence.

The improving sentences portion of the PSAT is designed to test your ability to identify the most correct and effective way to write a sentence. You will be presented with five answer choices, as described below. You should identify the choice that is

- Most clear and precise

- Least awkward or ambiguous

- Most effective in expression

You will be given questions similar to the ones that follow. There are four main strategies for dealing with improving sentences questions:

- *Read the sentence quickly but with care*, noting especially the underlined portion. Look for anything that strikes you as awkward or unclear in meaning—that is, look for "clunky" or "fuzzy" sentences.

- *"Speak" the sentence silently*, as you are apt to pick up any awkwardness of construction this way.

- *Trust yourself* if the sentence "sounds odd," even if you cannot pinpoint at first what is wrong.

- If the sentence strikes you as wrong somehow, *quickly revise it in your mind*. Then read the choices to see if your revision (or a similar one) is there. If it is, mark that choice and move on.

- *If the way the sentence is originally written is clearer and more effective than any of the revisions*, mark choice (A) and move on.

Try your hand at the following sentence:

> As a general rule of thumb, students are not allowed to go off campus, between the time they arrive at school in the morning and the time they return home at night.

(A)   (As it is now)

(B)   As a general rule of thumb, students are not allowed to go off campus during the day, between when they arrive and the time they go home.

(C)   Students are not allowed to go off campus during the school day.

(D)   Students are not allowed to go off campus, between the time they arrive at school in the morning and the time they return home at night.

(E)   Students are not allowed to go off campus, between arrival and departure time.

The correct answer is (C). It is clear and to the point and says all it needs to say. Your first strategy here is to note the cliché at the very beginning of the sentence—a clear indication that choice (A) is not the answer. Clichés often (though not always) indicate that the sentence is wordy. Choice (B) also contains the cliché and is wordy. Choice (D) has dropped the cliché, so it's better but still wordy. Choice (E) is vague, as it does not say to *whose arrival and departure time* it is referring.

> While riding a horse, an injury was sustained to the knee, and we had to go home early.

(A)   (As it is now)

(B)   an injury was sustained to my knee

(C)   my knee was injured

(D)   I injured my knee

(E)   I injured the knee

The correct answer is (D). A close look will show you that, in the original sentence, the real subject isn't present. (The injury seems to be riding the horse!) Your strategy here is to read the sentence quickly, then ask yourself why it seems vague. Choices (A), (B), and (C) are wrong because they are not subjects that can logically be modified by the phrase "while riding a horse." Choice (E) is wrong because, like the original version, it does not specify whose knee was injured.

Too much candy was given to the children by their aunt.

(A)   (As it is now)
(B)   The children, by their aunt, was given too much candy.
(C)   Their aunt gave the children too much candy.
(D)   Too much candy, by their aunt, was given to the children.
(E)   Candy given to the children by their aunt was excessive.

The correct answer is (C). The sentence as written makes ineffective use of the passive voice. An approach to this question would be to ask yourself why choice (A) sounds flat. It is because the person committing the action is not in the subject (or active) position in the sentence. Choices (B) and (D) are awkward. Choice (E) is unnecessarily convoluted.

The brothers Grimm, Jacob and Wilhelm, have inspired many myths, some of which were made up by their admirers.

(A)   (As it is now)
(B)   The brothers Grimm have inspired many myths, some made up by their admirers; their names were Jacob and Wilhelm.
(C)   Some myths, inspired by the brothers Grimm, Jacob and Wilhelm, were made up by their admirers.
(D)   The brothers Grimm, Jacob and Wilhelm, have inspired many myths, their admirers made up some of them.
(E)   Many myths made up by the admirers of the brothers Grimm, Jacob and Wilhelm, were inspired by them.

The correct answer is (A). The sentence is fine the way it is. Approach this problem by reading the sentence quickly, "speaking" it silently. You will find it rhythmical rather than "clunky." Now examine it for grammatical errors. There are none. Quickly read the choices just to make sure there isn't a better one. Choices (B) through (E) are all awkward. Choice (D) also has a comma splice.

EXERCISE

Directions: Part or all of the following numbered sentences are underlined. Beneath each are five choices. The first choice is to leave the sentence as is; the other four choices show ways to rephrase the underlined portions. The portions that are not underlined should remain the same. Choose the most effective version of each sentence.

1. By the time they arrived at 2 a.m., I was so worried I was fixing to call the police.

   (A) (As it is now)
   (B) I am calling the police
   (C) I am about to call the police
   (D) I was about to call the police
   (E) I'm geared up to call the police

2. She is hurrying as fast as she can, and I believe she's too late.

   (A) (As it is now)
   (B) or
   (C) but
   (D) moreover
   (E) also

3. The heat in the desert was unbearable by day, although at night we were comfortably cool.

   (A) (As it is now)
   (B) day; although
   (C) day! Although
   (D) day. Although
   (E) day? Although

4. My Aunt Jody's cake was as good, maybe better than my mom's.

   (A) (As it is now)
   (B) as good as, maybe better than, my mom's
   (C) good as my mom's, maybe better.
   (D) as good over my mom's, maybe better
   (E) as good, maybe gooder, than my mom's

ANSWERS AND EXPLANATIONS

1. **The correct answer is (D).** Choices (A) and (E) represent a shift from formal to informal diction. Choices (B) and (C) represent a shift in tense from past to present.

2. **The correct answer is (C).** The other choices are examples of faulty coordination.

3. **The correct answer is (A).** Choice (B) is incorrect, because a semicolon should separate two independent clauses, and here the second clause is made dependent by use of the subordinator *although*. Choices (C), (D), and (E) are incorrect because they turn the second clause into a sentence fragment.

4. **The correct answer is (B).** Choices (A) and (C) have parts missing. Choices (D) and (E) are unidiomatic.

IMPROVING PARAGRAPHS

The improving paragraphs section of the PSAT is designed to test your ability to make choices that will

- Improve the logic of a flawed passage

- Improve the coherence of a flawed passage

- Improve the organization of a flawed passage

In the improving paragraphs section, you will be given the early draft of a short essay, each sentence of which will be numbered. Some parts of the essay will need to be revised. For each question, you will be given five choices and asked to pick the best revision. One of the choices may be to leave the part in question alone.

Following are suggestions on how to approach an improving paragraphs question:

- Read the whole essay quickly to get the *overall sense* of it. Do not linger on the errors—these are what you will be asked questions about.

- Pay close attention to the *context* of the sentence or paragraph in question, making sure that your revision (if any) makes sense in terms of the whole essay.

- Choose the *best answer* from the five choices, even if you can think of a better revision than the ones offered.

Following is a short passage, such as you might find on the PSAT, followed by questions you might be confronted with. Read the passage and answer the questions that come after it. Some of the questions will ask you to improve sentence structure and word choice. Other questions will refer to parts of the essay or to the entire essay and will ask you to improve organization and development.

(1) *The following Federal Aviation Administration rules shall apply to parachute jumps over or into congested areas of open air assemblies of persons, for the safety of parachutists and of persons on the ground.*
(2) *No person may make a parachute jump over or into a congested area of a city, town, or settlement, or an open air assembly of persons unless a certificate of authorization for that jump has been issued to that person.*
(3) *A parachutist may drift over that congested area or open air assembly with a fully deployed and properly functioning parachute if he or she is at a*

44

sufficient altitude to avoid creating a hazard to persons and property on the ground. (4) Unless prior approval has been given by the airport management, no person may make any parachute jump over an airport that does not have a functioning control tower operated by the United States or onto any airport. (5) However, a parachutist may drift over that airport with a fully deployed and properly functioning parachute. (6) This is allowed to occur only if he or she is at least 2,000 feet above that airport's traffic pattern and avoids creating a hazard to air traffic or to persons and property on the ground.

(7) An application for a certificate of authorization can be made in a form and in a manner prescribed by the Administrator and you will submit it to the Federal Aviation Administration Flight Standards District Office having jurisdiction over the area in which the parachute jump is to be made, at least four days before the day of that jump.

In the context of the passage, which of the following topics would most logically be addressed after sentence (6)?

(A) A history of parachuting in the United States
(B) How to get prior approval from the airport management
(C) The history of the parachute in the United States
(D) The purpose of FAA rules and regulations
(E) The definition of *traffic pattern* and how it is planned

The correct answer is (B). In the second paragraph, the topic of getting a certificate of authorization for parachute jumping is discussed, and, following that, the topic of getting prior approval from the airport management for jumping. It is logical to follow the same sequence in the third paragraph, in which obtaining these two types of authorization is discussed. Choices (A), (C), and (E) are irrelevant to the main purpose of the passage, which is how parachute jumping is regulated. Choice (D) is explained in the first paragraph.

In context, which is the best transition between the underlined portions of sentences (2) and (3) reproduced below?

to that person. (3) A parachutist

(A) to that person. Therefore, a parachutist
(B) to that person. However, a parachutist
(C) to that person. Hereafter, a parachutist
(D) to that person. Anyhow, a parachutist
(E) to that person. Whereupon, a parachutist

The correct answer is (B). The other transitions are illogical.

In context, which is the best version of the underlined portion of sentence (7) reproduced below?

An application for a certificate of authorization can be made in a form and in a manner prescribed by the Administrator and you will submit it to the Federal Aviation Administration Flight Standards District Office having jurisdiction over the area in which the parachute jump is to be made, at least four days before the day of that jump.

(A) (As it is now)
(B) and must be submitted
(C) and which must be submitted
(D) having been submitted
(E) will have been submitted

The correct answer is (B). Choice (A) represents a shift in person from third to second. The phrase *and which* makes choice (C) ungrammatical. Choices (D) and (E) represent a shift in tense.

In the context of the passage, which of the following is the best way to revise and combine the underlined portions of sentences (5) and (6) reproduced below?

parachute. (6) This is allowed to occur

(A) parachute if and only if they are
(B) parachute and he or she is
(C) parachute whenever he or she is
(D) parachute so he or she is
(E) parachute if he or she is

The correct answer is (E). In choice (A), the phrase *and only if* makes the sentence wordy. In choices (B), (C), and (D), the transitional words *whenever, so,* and *if* make the sentences illogical.

EXERCISE

> **DIRECTIONS:** Read the passage below and answer the questions that come after it. Some of the questions will ask you to improve sentence structure and word choice. Other questions will refer to parts of the essay or to the entire essay and ask you to improve organization and development.

(1) *El Niño was originally recognized by fishermen who were fishing off the coast of South America who noticed an appearance that was unusual of some unusually warm water in the Pacific Ocean, occurring very near the beginning or start of the year.* (2) *El Niño means The Little One in Spanish.*

(3) *El Niño is a disruption of the ocean-atmosphere system in the tropical Pacific having important consequences for weather around the world.* (4) *Among these consequences are increased rainfall across the southern tier of the United States and in Peru, which has caused destructive flooding and drought in the west Pacific, sometimes associated with devastating brushfires in Australia.* (5) *Its current is warm and poor in nutrients, and it kills plankton.* (6) *This forces larger organisms to starve.* (7) *Between 1982 and 1983, one of the worst El Niños in recorded history killed kelp forests in the upper levels of the ocean.* (8) *This resulted in a major loss of seabirds and serious devastation to the local Pacific food chain.*

1. In the context of the paragraph, which is the best version of sentence (1)?

   (A) (As it is now)

   (B) Originally being recognized by fishermen off the coast of South America as an appearance of some unusually warm water, occurring very near the beginning or the start of the year; El Niño was in the Pacific Ocean.

   (C) El Niño was originally recognized by fishermen off the coast of South America as the appearance of unusually warm water in the Pacific Ocean, occurring near the beginning of the year.

   (D) Occurring near the beginning of the year, some fishermen originally recognized El Niño as the appearance of some unusually warm water, it occurred very near the beginning of the year, in the Pacific Ocean.

   (E) Some fishermen originally recognized off the coast of South America, as an appearance of unusually warm water, occurring near the very beginning or start of this year in the Pacific Ocean.

2. Which of the following sentences, if true, would best follow sentence (2)?

   (A) This name was used because of its tendency to arrive around Christmas.

   (B) Arriving around Christmas, the name was used for the phenomenon because of this.

   (C) This name was used because of the tendency of the phenomenon to arrive around Christmas.

   (D) Its arrival around Christmas caused the phenomenon to have this name.

   (E) The name is totally appropriate because of the time that El Niño tends to arrive in December.

3. In sentence (4) the phrase *these consequences* refers to

   (A) weather around the world.

   (B) increased rainfall.

   (C) El Niño.

   (D) disruption of the ocean-atmosphere system in the South Pacific.

   (E) unusually warm currents in the Pacific Ocean.

4. In sentence (8), the word *This* refers to

   (A) an El Niño.

   (B) the major loss of seabirds.

   (C) the killing of kelp forests.

   (D) the starving of larger organisms.

   (E) the years 1982 and 1983.

5. In the context of the passage, which of the following is the best way to revise and combine the underlined portion of sentences (5) and (6) reproduced below?

   Its current is warm and poor in nutrients, and it kills plankton. (6) This forces larger organisms to starve.

   (A) it is killing plankton and forced

   (B) it kills plankton and it forced

   (C) it kills plankton, forcing

   (D) it will be killing plankton, forcing

   (E) it will have killed plankton, that forces

6. Which topic would most logically come next if the essay were continued?

   (A) The measures taken to predict El Niño in the areas usually worst hit

   (B) Description of the first El Niño in recorded history

   (C) Further detail about the brushfires in Australia

   (D) A listing of the categories of seabirds killed by El Niño between 1982 and 1983

   (E) Explanation of what is meant by the phrase *Pacific food chain*

ANSWERS AND EXPLANATIONS

1. **The correct answer is (C).** This is the least awkward and wordy of the five choices. Choice (A) is incorrect because it is wordy; there is no reason to write *fishermen who were fishing*, as this is redundant. Choice (B) is incorrect because the main idea of the sentence (the definition of El Niño as *unusually warm water*) is put into an awkward subordinate clause. Choice (D) is a comma splice. Choice (E) is grammatical; however, it is awkwardly constructed and wordy. Especially, there is no need to write *very beginning or start*, as this is redundant.

2. **The correct answer is (C).** Choice (A) is incorrect because *its* is a faulty pronoun reference, seeming to refer to *name*. Choice (B) is incorrect because *Arriving around Christmas* is a misplaced modifier, seeming to modify *name* rather than El Niño. Choice (D) is incorrect because *its* is a vague pronoun reference. Choice (E) is incorrect because it is wordy. Also, the use of the word *totally* is a shift in style from formal to informal.

3. **The correct answer is (B).** It eliminates all the other choices.

4. **The correct answer is (C).** If we substitute each choice in place of the pronoun, no other choice fits.

5. **The correct answer is (C).** The other choices represent a shift in tense.

6. **The correct answer is (A).** The main focus of the passage is the destructive effects of El Niño; therefore, measures taken to predict this destructive force are most relevant and would most logically come next. The other choices are marginally related to the main topic but are all too narrow.

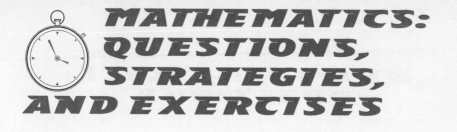

MATHEMATICS: QUESTIONS, STRATEGIES, AND EXERCISES

There are two Mathematics sections on the PSAT, each allowing you 25 minutes to complete. Thirty of the forty math questions are multiple choice, and ten are student-produced responses.

This book will explain each type of math question, its directions, and what abilities each type is testing. You will be provided with examples, tips, and strategies, as well as the chance to practice all kinds of questions. Every item is designed to encourage your success on the PSAT.

As on the real test, you will be answering questions about arithmetic, algebra, and geometry. Some of the items will remind you of exercises in your math textbooks, where you are asked to use numeric, spatial, graphic, symbolic, and logic skills. Other items may seem innovative to you. They will present original situations that require combining the tools you have learned with imaginative problem solving.

About Calculators

You may use a four-function, scientific, or graphing calculator on the two math sections of the PSAT. In fact, you are encouraged to bring one, even if you don't think you will use it. Be sure to take a calculator you have practiced with.

No PSAT question will *require* a calculator. However, studies show that students who use calculators do slightly better in scoring than those who don't. On most problems, you probably won't need a calculator. The best course is to decide first how you are going to solve each question, and then decide as you go whether to use your calculator to save time.

MULTIPLE-CHOICE QUESTIONS

There will be twenty multiple-choice math questions on your PSAT, comprising Section 2 of the test. These questions require you to read a problem carefully, determine just what is being asked, use math skills and/or reasoning to solve the problem, and fill in one of the five possible answers on your answer sheet.

However, PSAT math questions do more than test your knowledge and skills in arithmetic, algebra, and geometry. They are also designed to test your application of knowledge to new situations. Some problems test reasoning and deduction.

Tips for Answering Multiple-Choice Questions

- Keep in mind that on a multiple-choice question, *the correct answer will always be there* (even if it is "none of these"). You just have to eliminate the wrong answers to find it.

- *Estimate answers.* For example, you might round off all numbers, say to the closest power of 10, and estimate the answer. Estimation, when appropriate, can help you save time on computations.

- *Use the process of elimination.* Wrong answers are often easier to find than the right answer.

- *Write down formulas on your test booklet* so you use them correctly.

- *When plugging in numbers to expressions with variables or unknowns in them (x), substitute both positive and negative values, zero, and fractions as values,* unless the directions define the term otherwise (for example, $x > 0$).

- *Don't worry if you can't answer every question.* Very few people can. Work carefully on those you can answer, and, if you skip a problem, be sure to skip the corresponding row on the answer sheet.

- *Keep practicing!* The more you practice, the more comfortable you will be with the PSAT format and the skills it tests.

Study these directions, which closely resemble the ones you will find on the PSAT, then try answering the questions that follow.

Directions: This section consists of multiple-choice problems, each of which has five possible answers. Solve each problem. Then decide which is the best of the choices given.

In which, if any, of the following can the 3's be divided out without changing the value of the expression?

(A) $3e - 3f$

(B) $\dfrac{3e - f}{3}$

(C) $\dfrac{e^3}{f^3}$

(D) $\dfrac{\frac{e}{3}}{\frac{f}{3}}$

(E) none of these

The correct answer is (D). Substitute two low-valued integers for e and f. Don't plug in 0 because its unique properties will complicate the comparisons. Instead, let $e = 2$ and $f = 1$, and evaluate each expression before and after dividing out the 3's.

	Expression	*Before*		*After*
(A)	$3e - 3f$	$3(2) - 3(1) = 3$	$\neq$	$2 - 1 = 1$
(B)	$\dfrac{3e - f}{3}$	$\dfrac{3(2) - (1)}{3} = \dfrac{5}{3}$	$\neq$	$\dfrac{2 - 1}{3} = \dfrac{1}{3}$
(C)	$\dfrac{e^3}{f^3}$	$\dfrac{2^3}{1^3} = \dfrac{8}{1} = 8$	$\neq$	$\dfrac{2}{1} = 2$
(D)	$\dfrac{\frac{e}{3}}{\frac{f}{3}}$	$\dfrac{\frac{2}{3}}{\frac{1}{3}} = \dfrac{2}{1} = 2$	$=$	$\dfrac{2}{1} = 2$

The correct answer is (D). It is the only choice where both expressions work.

When solving a PSAT math problem that seems confusing or complex, ask yourself three questions:

1. What information is given?

2. What am I asked to find?

3. What is the relationship between these two things?

In this case, you are given four expressions and asked to find if any of them remain the same after a certain change (dividing out the 3's). You need to substitute for the unknowns in order to compare the "before and after" of each expression to see if their relationship is "equal."

> In a box that contains only red and yellow hard candies, the ratio of red to yellow is 2:3. What is the probability of randomly selecting a yellow candy?
>
> (A) $\dfrac{2}{5}$
>
> (B) $\dfrac{1}{2}$
>
> (C) $\dfrac{3}{5}$
>
> (D) $\dfrac{2}{3}$
>
> (E) $\dfrac{3}{4}$

The correct answer is (C). Let P = the probability of a yellow candy being selected. Then let $2x$ be the number of red candies in the box and $3x$ be the number of yellow candies:

$$P = \frac{3x}{2x + 3x} = \frac{3x}{5x} = \frac{3}{5}$$

The probability of a yellow candy being randomly selected is 3 out of 5. Your choice should be (C).

Remember that when letters stand for numbers, the same arithmetic operations can be performed on them. Think of how you would solve the problem with numbers and perform the same operations on variables. For example, in this problem you combine like terms ($2x + 3x$) and you simplify a fraction (by dividing out the common x's).

Refer to the figure below when answering the next question.

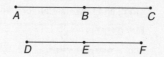

If $AB > DE$ and $BC > EF$, then

(A) $DF > AC$
(B) $AC > DF$
(C) $AB + EF = BC + DE$
(D) $AB + BC < DE + EF$
(E) $AB + DE = BC + EF$

The correct answer is (B). The only answer among these five that you can be 100 percent sure of with the givens you have in this problem is that $AC > DF$. All the other answer choices are assuming that points B and E are midpoints of the larger segments.

Recall that with inequalities, the whole is always greater than its parts, so line segment AC will be greater than either of its parts, AB or BC, and line segment DF will be greater than either DE or EF.

Second, since $AB > DE$ and $BC > EF$, the sum of the first two segments will also be greater than the sum of the second two segments. This is the rule for inequalities that states "if unequal quantities are added to unequal quantities of the same order, the resulting sums are unequal in the same order." Or, if $x > y$ and $a > b$, then $x + a > y + b$.

Points B and E look to be midpoints of the two segments, and that is why this problem is challenging. They may or may not be midpoints; you are not told. Warning: You cannot assume any more than you are given!

Study the chart below, then answer the question that follows.

High and Low Rainfall for Five Months

For which month was the difference between the low rainfall and the high rainfall the greatest?

- **(A)** January
- **(B)** February
- **(C)** March
- **(D)** April
- **(E)** May

The correct answer is (D). You'll note from the legend that the longer bar (shown second for each month) represents the highest rainfall in that month. The first bar is the lowest rainfall.

You are asked which month has the greatest difference in high and low rainfall, so you are actually comparing the parts of the lower bars that extend beyond the upper bars. By comparing these sections, you know that the month with the greatest difference is April, choice (D). If you are unsure about this, you can numerically check the difference between the two bars in each month. In April, the difference is $9 - 5$, or about 4 inches. The next closest difference is in February, choice (B), which is 3.5 inches.

If your test question has a graphic, such as this bar chart, scan it first. Read the title, the legend, and the labels so you will know what the graphic represents and compares. You may have to compute figures, or you may be able to eyeball the graphic and deduce the answer without doing any figuring at all.

EXERCISE

1. What is the maximum number of sections a circle can be divided into by 4 chords?

   (A) 4
   (B) 8
   (C) 10
   (D) 11
   (E) 12

2. $\left(3\sqrt{8}\right)\left(2\sqrt{18}\right) =$

   (A) $5\sqrt{26}$
   (B) $6\sqrt{12}$
   (C) 72
   (D) 144
   (E) 156

3. Name the first of four consecutive odd integers where the sum of the greatest and twice the least is 27.

   (A) 3
   (B) 5
   (C) 7
   (D) 9
   (E) 11

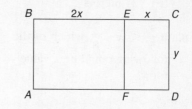

4. In the figure above, the area of rectangle *ABCD* is how many times as great as the area of rectangle *FECD*?

   (A) 2
   (B) 3
   (C) 6
   (D) 12
   (E) It cannot be determined from the information given.

5. $(125 \times 115) + (172 \times 125) + (125 \times 113) =$

   (A) 40,000
   (B) 46,000
   (C) 48,000
   (D) 49,000
   (E) 50,000

6. What is the average length, in inches, of three boards of the following lengths: 18 inches, 1.25 feet, and $1\frac{2}{3}$ yard?

   (A) 18
   (B) 31
   (C) 36
   (D) 82
   (E) 93

7. If the area of a square is 36 square meters, what is its perimeter?

(A) 16 meters
(B) 18 meters
(C) 20 meters
(D) 22 meters
(E) 24 meters

8. If $\frac{4}{5} < x < \frac{7}{8}$, which of the following could be a value for x?

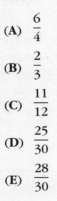

(A) $\frac{6}{4}$

(B) $\frac{2}{3}$

(C) $\frac{11}{12}$

(D) $\frac{25}{30}$

(E) $\frac{28}{30}$

9. A baker's helper earns 9 dollars per hour, including lunch and break time. This week, he works from 4 a.m. to noon on Monday, Tuesday, and Friday and from 5 a.m. to 11 a.m. on Wednesday and Thursday. How much money did the baker's helper earn this week?

(A) $36
(B) $216
(C) $324
(D) $350
(E) $369

10. At Boulder High, $\frac{6}{10}$ of the students are old enough to drive. Of these students, $\frac{1}{3}$ drive their own cars to school each day. What percent of the students at Boulder High drive their own cars to school every day?

(A) 20%
(B) 25%
(C) 33%
(D) 50%
(E) 82%

ANSWERS AND EXPLANATIONS

1. **The correct answer is (D).** First, you need to be familiar with certain vocabulary, such as *maximum* (the greatest amount) and *chord* (a line segment connecting any two points on a circle). If you don't understand a term, you often may be able to figure it out by its context in the sentence. (For example, "divided into" suggests that a chord cuts across the circle.)

   If you start sketching this problem, you should see that the greatest number of sections will occur when each of the 4 chords only intersects another chord in one place. In other words, no *three* chords should intersect at the same point. There are infinite combinations of these lines, but the greatest number of sections they can make is 11, choice (D).

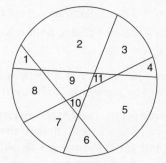

   As you saw in this problem, sketching is an excellent way to test a problem by trial and error. No one will see the sketches or notes you put on your test booklet, so draw as much as you want to "get the picture" when the words are not clear enough.

2. **The correct answer is (C).** Multiply the outer integers (3×2) first; then multiply the numbers within the square roots together, $\left(\sqrt{8} \times \sqrt{18}\right)$ and simplify:

$$\left(3\sqrt{8}\right)\left(2\sqrt{18}\right) = 6\left(\sqrt{8} \times \sqrt{18}\right) = 6\sqrt{144} = (6)(12) = 72$$

   When considering roots, remember that if there is no superscript number inside the radical sign (called the *index*), then the number two is assumed to be the index. In other words, the symbol $\sqrt{}$ always means *square root*, not cube root or any other.

3. **The correct answer is (C).** This problem can be confusing, so it is especially important to be clear on the answer to "What am I asked to find?" You are asked to find the first (which is also the least) of four particular consecutive odd integers. Let the first number be n. Since n is odd, adding 2 to n will give you the next consecutive odd number and so on.

Therefore, n, $n + 2$, $n + 4$, and $n + 6$ are the consecutive integers, with the least being n and the greatest being $n + 6$. You are told that the greatest integer plus twice the least is 27. Translate this information into an equation:

$$(n + 6) + 2n = 27 \qquad \text{Combine like terms.}$$
$$3n + 6 = 27 \qquad \text{Subtract 6 from both sides.}$$
$$3n = 21 \qquad \text{Divide both sides by 3.}$$
$$n = 7$$

Double-check that your answer is what was asked for—the least of the four numbers. It is. The answer is 7, choice (C).

4. **The correct answer is (B).** Look at the givens in the diagram. Even if you didn't know if the picture was drawn to scale, you do know that rectangles *ABCD* and *FECD* share one side with a measurement of y. And you know that one side of interior rectangle *ABEF* is measured as $2x$ and the corresponding side of interior rectangle *FECD* is called x. Add the two lengths together to get $2x + x = 3x$. The largest rectangle is then 3 times the size of the smaller interior rectangle.

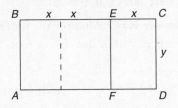

Another technique is to draw a line dividing rectangle *ABEF* into two equal, x by y, rectangles, to see that a total 3 of these rectangles, x by y, fit into *ABCD*.

5. **The correct answer is (E).** Look each math problem over briefly before you start doing the math. In this case, you will notice that 125 is a repeated factor, so factor it out: $125(115 + 172 + 113)$. Add the numbers within the parentheses, then multiply their sum by 125 on your calculator. $125(400) = 50,000$, choice (E).

   Factoring, rounding, and estimating are all helpful shortcuts to practice before you take the real PSAT.

6. **The correct answer is (B).** When you work a problem, especially finding an average or making a comparison, be sure that all the units of measurement are the same. In this case, you will have to convert the lengths of all three pieces of wood into the smallest common unit, which is inches:

   The first board is 18 inches.

   The second board is 1.25 feet or $1\frac{1}{4}$ feet $= 12 + \frac{1}{4}(12) = 15$ inches.

   The third board is $1\frac{2}{3}$ yard $= 36 + \frac{2}{3}(36) = 60$ inches.

   The total is 93 inches, choice (E). But is this the answer you are asked for? No! You now need to figure the average length of the boards: $93 \div 3 = 31$, choice (B). The remaining choices did not do the unit conversions correctly.

7. **The correct answer is (E).** The formula for the area of a square is $A = s^2$, so $s = \sqrt{36} = 6$. The formula for the perimeter is $P = 4s$, which means the perimeter of the square is $P = (4)(6) = 24$.

8. **The correct answer is (D).** It could be a good idea to use your calculator here. Renaming the inequality from fractions as decimals will make comparison easier and reduce the chances of error. The inequality thus becomes $.800 < x < .875$. Now, you can immediately rule out the first two because choice (A), $\frac{6}{4}$, is obviously much greater than $\frac{7}{8}$, and choice (B), $\frac{2}{3}$, is much less than $\frac{4}{5}$. Here is where it pays to have memorized the most common fractional equivalents in decimals. The last three choices are best tackled with your calculator. After renaming them as decimals, it is easy to spot choice (D), $\frac{25}{30}$ or $.8\overline{3}3$, as the answer.

9. **The correct answer is (C).** The helper's hours are:

$$8 \text{ hrs each day on Mon., Tues., and Fri.} = (8)(3) = 24 \text{ hrs}$$
$$6 \text{ hrs each day on Wed. and Thurs.} = (6)(2) = \underline{12 \text{ hrs}}$$
$$\text{Total hours worked} = 36 \text{ hrs}$$

This week the helper earned ($9/hr)(36 hrs) = $324

10. **The correct answer is (A).** You can think of this one as a problem that calculates a percentage of the percentage. To get the answer, you don't even need to know the total number of students at Boulder High, just figure out what $\frac{1}{3}$ of $\frac{6}{10}$ is, and you're all set. First, rename $\frac{6}{10}$ as .6 and $\frac{1}{3}$ as $.3\overline{3}$, then translate the words into an equation:

Percent of students who drive their cars to school $= (.3\overline{3})(.6) \approx .198$, about 20%

WORD PROBLEMS

A word problem can be looked at as a little story told with numbers or variables (that is, a letter that represents an unknown number). At the end of the story, you are asked a question.

Example

Jochim spent $17 at the food court in the mall on Saturday, whereas Milton (who had four extra orders of fries) spent $23. How much more did Milton spend at the food court than Jochim?

Word problems are found in all types of math, from arithmetic to algebra to geometry.

To approach word problems, take the following steps:

1. Read in small segments, rather than trying to make sense of the whole problem at once. <u>Underline</u> each important segment—this will help you separate the math problem from the story.

   <u>Jochim spent $17</u> at the Food Court in the Mall on Saturday, whereas <u>Milton</u> (who had four extra orders of fries) <u>spent $23</u>. How much more did Milton spend at the Food Court than Jochim?

   (A) $6
   (B) $15
   (C) $23
   (D) $30
   (E) $40

   The correct answer is (A). $23 − $17 = $6.

2. If the problem is a complex one, you might want to **circle the question**, just to help you keep in mind what you're looking for.

3. For multiple-choice questions, **look over the answers** before you begin working the problem. Work in fractions if the answer is in fractions, and in decimals if the answer choices are in decimals.

4. DON'T fall for the most obvious answer choice—**work the problem**, even if you're sure what the outcome will be. In the above example, you're not likely to get confused, but if the problem were larger and more complex, you MIGHT, in haste, choose the *sum* of the numbers, choice (E), rather than the *difference* between them. Test-writers love to include answers that seem right but aren't.

5. **Check your answer.** Again, it could match one of the choices but still be wrong.

As is the case with arithmetic, word problems in algebra tell a little story, this time requiring you to translate the words into algebraic expressions. Word problems test not only your math skills, but also your ability to reason. When working with word problems, proceed systematically as follows:

- Read carefully to be sure you understand the problem.

- Understand what you are being asked to solve for.

- Figure out what information you are given.

- Figure out what information you need.

- Decide how to solve the problem.

- Solve the problem.

- Check your answer to make sure it answers the question.

If you become familiar with the key words and phrases used in word problems, they will be much easier to solve. It's a good idea to memorize these words along with their algebraic translations because they are used often on the PSAT:

The Words	The Translation	Example
Is, has, was	=	Jill **is** three years older.
Sum of, greater than, more than, further than	+	A town is 5 miles **further than**
Difference, less than, fewer, younger than	−	The cost is $1.75 **less than**
Of what number?	%	20 is $\frac{1}{5}$ **of** what number?
$\frac{2}{3}$ of a tank of gas	×	The car used $\frac{2}{3}$ **of** a tank of gas.
Per, for hour	÷	Hiking at 3 miles **per** hour
shoes sold **for** every hat	ratio	3 pair of shoes **for**

Sample Word Problem

48 is 80 percent of what number?

- Read the problem carefully.

- You are being asked to find a number; let's call it x. We want to solve for x.

- We are given two pieces of information: 48 and what it represents, 80% of x.

- We have enough information to solve the problem once we translate it into algebra.

  The translation is: $48 = 80\%$ of x

  $\qquad\qquad\qquad 48 = .80x$

- Solve the problem: $x = \dfrac{48}{.80}$ or $x = 60$

- Check your answer: 60 makes sense, answers the question, and checks $(.80)(60) = 48$.

EXERCISE

> **DIRECTIONS:** This section consists of multiple-choice problems, each of which has five possible answers. Solve each problem. Then decide which is the best of the choices given.

1. If a hiker can travel at a steady rate of 15 minutes per $\frac{3}{4}$ mile, how many hours would it take to walk 9 miles?

   (A) 1.8
   (B) 2
   (C) 3
   (D) 4
   (E) 6.75

2. The perimeter of a circular building measures 158 feet. What is the approximate radius of the building's outer wall?

   (A) 7
   (B) 25
   (C) 50
   (D) 76
   (E) 101

3. The price of admission to a movie theater has increased 15%. If a ticket originally cost 5 dollars, what is the new price?

   (A) $4.25
   (B) $5.25
   (C) $5.75
   (D) $6.25
   (E) $6.75

4. The net price of a television set is $306 after successive discounts of 15% and 10% off the marked price. What is the marked price?

   (A) $234.09
   (B) $400
   (C) $382.50
   (D) $408
   (E) None of the above

5. A woman's coin purse contains 65 cents in 11 coins, all nickels and dimes. How many coins are dimes?

   (A) 1
   (B) 2
   (C) 3
   (D) 4
   (E) 5

6. A year ago, Tom and Al each deposited $1,000 in separate investment accounts. Tom's account earns 5% every year. Al's account earns 2.5% every six months. What is the difference between Tom's and Al's accounts today?

   (A) $0
   (B) $0.63
   (C) $25.63
   (D) $25
   (E) $50

ANSWERS AND EXPLANATIONS

1. **The correct answer is (C).** First, convert 15 minutes to hours to make the units of measurement match, 15 minutes = .25 hour. In this case, it is easier to work with decimals, so convert also $\frac{3}{4}$ mile = .75 mile. Now set up the following proportion and solve for x:

$$\frac{.25\text{hr}}{.75\text{mi}} = \frac{x\text{hr}}{9\text{mi}}$$

$$(.75)x = (.25)(9)$$

$$x = (.25)(9) \div (.75)$$

$$x = 3\text{hrs}$$

2. **The correct answer is (B).** The circumference of a circle is $C = 2\pi r$. We are given $C = 158$, so we have:

$$158 = 2\pi r$$

or

$$r = 158 \div 2\pi$$

$$r \approx 25$$

3. **The correct answer is (C).** To solve this one, just add 15% of the original ticket price to the original ticket price.

$$\text{New Price} = 5 + 15\% \text{ of } 5$$

$$= 5 + (.15)(5)$$

$$= 5 + .75$$

$$= 5.75$$

4. **The correct answer is (B).** If marked price = m, first sale price = $.85m$ and net price = $.90\,(.85)m = .765m$.

$$.765m = 306$$

$$m = 400$$

Or work from the answer choices: 15% of $400 = $60, making a first sale price of $340. 10% of this price is $34, making the net price $306.

5. **The correct answer is (B).** Solve this one by translating the word into an algebraic relationship. We know the coins are only nickels or dimes. Of the 11 coins, we are asked to find x, the number of dimes. This means there are x dimes and $(11 - x)$ nickels. Now translate this information into algebraic form:

$.65$ = (value of a dime)(number of dimes) + (value of a nickel) (number of nickels)

$$= (.10)x + (.05)(11 - x)$$
$$= .10x + .55 - .05x$$
$$= (.10 - .05)x + .55$$
$$= .05x + .55$$
$$.05x = .65 - .55$$
$$x = \frac{.10}{.05}$$
$$x = 2$$

6. **The correct answer is (B).** After one year, Tom has: $1,000 + (.05)(1,000) = \$1,050$. After one year, Al has: $1,000 + (.025)(1,000) + (.025)(1025) = \$1,050.63$. This makes the difference between two accounts: $\$1,050.63 - \$1,050 = \$0.63$.

STUDENT-PRODUCED RESPONSES

The second Mathematics section of the PSAT includes eight problems that are called student-produced responses. In this set, you are asked to solve each problem, marking its answer in ovals on a provided grid. The student-produced responses are designed to test your ability to solve a math problem on your own, without the advantage of the process of elimination.

The student-produced responses portion of your answer sheet will have eight answer grids. Each grid consists of four columns and twelve rows. To enter a number onto the grid, write each of its digits or symbols in exact order in the boxes at the top of the grid. Then shade in the corresponding oval beneath it. A decimal point is provided for numbers such as .25, and a slash is provided for fractions, such as $\frac{1}{4}$. The PSAT grading machine will read only the filled-in ovals, not your writing in the boxes at the top of the grid.

Study these directions, which closely resemble the ones you will find on the PSAT:

Directions: This section consists of student-produced responses, which require you to solve a problem and enter your answer by marking the ovals on the special grid.

The following are examples of correctly entered numbers:

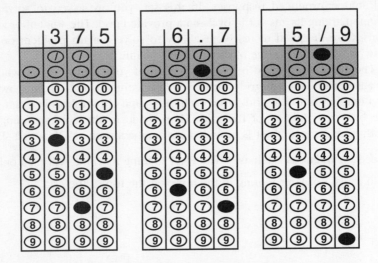

You may start your answers in any column, space permitting. Columns should be left blank if they are not needed.

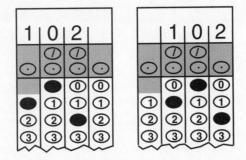

Tips for Gridding-In Your Answers

Remember the following when entering numbers onto the answer grid:

- Although not required, it is suggested that you *begin by writing your answer in the boxes at the top.* Doing this will help you grid-in the ovals accurately.

- *Mark no more than one oval in any one column.*

- The answer sheet will be machine scored on the real PSAT, so *you will only receive credit if the ovals are filled in correctly.*

- Some problems may have more than one correct answer; if this is the case, *grid-in only one answer.*

- *No question will have a negative answer.*

- *If your answer is a fraction, you must grid-in the fraction slash in its own column.*

- *If your answer contains a decimal point, you must enter it in its own column.*

- *Mixed numbers, such as* $1\frac{1}{2}$, *must be gridded-in using either a decimal point (1.5) or an improper fraction* $\left(\frac{3}{2}\right)$. If you enter your answer as a mixed number, the machine scoring your test will interpret 11/2 as $\frac{11}{2}$, not $1\frac{1}{2}$.

- *If your solution is a repeating decimal, such as 0.6666 . . . , you must round the number to the most accurate answer the grid can accommodate (such as .666 or .667).* Less accurate values, such as .6 or .67, will not be correct.

Now try answering a few student-produced response problems. (Note: You will have a chance to practice entering answers on the answer grid when you do the exercise on page 75.)

What is 60% expressed as a fraction?

The correct answer is $\frac{3}{5}$. $60\% = \frac{60}{100}$. Simplify the fraction: $\frac{60}{100} = \frac{6}{10} = \frac{3}{5}$. On the PSAT, don't forget to grid-in the fraction slash in its own column.

Practice renaming percentages, fractions, and decimals. Remember that a percentage is just another way to express a fraction whose denominator is 100.

To Rename . . .

a percentage as a fraction . . .	put the percentage (without the percent sign) over a denominator of 100 and simplify the fraction.
a fraction as a percentage . . .	divide the numerator by the denominator and move the decimal point in the result two places to the right.
a percentage as a decimal . . .	move the decimal point two places to the left.
a decimal as a percentage . . .	move the decimal point two places to the right.

Try another problem:

What is $3 \times [7 - (6 \div 3)^2]$?

The answer is 9. Clear the parentheses first, by dividing 6 by 3, to get 2. Then square that number to get $2^2 = 4$. Next, clear the brackets by subtracting: $7 - 4 = 3$; and finally multiply 3×3 to get your answer of 9.

Often on the PSAT you will need to perform more than one math operation. As you know, there are six operations: addition, subtraction, multiplication, division, raising to a power, and finding a square or cube root. These operations must be performed in the correct order: first clear the parentheses and brackets by taking care of the operations inside them; then take care of the exponents or roots; then multiply, divide, add, and subtract.

Some students think of the acronym PEMDAS, which stands for Parentheses, Exponents, Multiplication, Division, Addition, and Subtraction to help them remember the order of operations.

What is the area of a two-foot-wide path around a rectangular swimming pool that is 40 feet long and 20 feet wide?

The correct answer is 256. There are two methods to figuring this problem, but drawing a sketch of the pool and its path is very helpful to either method.

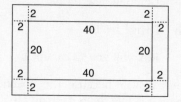

Method 1: Find the area of the pool and the area of the pool and the path together. Subtract the lesser from the greater.

Area of the pool = $40 \times 20 = 800$ sq ft

Area of the pool and the path together = $(40 + 2 + 2)$
$\times (20 + 2 + 2) = 44 \times 24 = 1{,}056$ sq ft

Area of the path alone = $1{,}056 - 800 = 256$ sq ft

Method 2: Divide the path into knowable areas and add those together. As you see in your sketch, the path consists of

$$
\begin{aligned}
2 \text{ rectangles that are } 40 \times 2 &= 2(40 \times 2) = 160 \text{ sq ft} \\
2 \text{ rectangles that are } 20 \times 2 &= 2(20 \times 2) = \ 80 \text{ sq ft} \\
4 \text{ squares that are } 2 \times 2 &= 4(2 \times 2) = \underline{\ 16 \text{ sq ft}} \\
& \qquad\qquad\qquad\quad 256 \text{ sq ft}
\end{aligned}
$$

To solve a PSAT problem, you may have to look at the larger picture broken down to its basic parts as in Method 2, where the path is divided into the rectangles and squares.

As you see, a problem can often be approached in more than one way. Choose the quickest and clearest method for you, and keep practicing. Rewrite the problems you have trouble with, using different numbers, and practice the same skills to arrive at new answers. The more you practice problems like the ones in this book, the more comfortable you will be with the PSAT format and the skills it tests.

Drew, Lee, and Rex are dividing up 320 caramels in this way: Drew gets four times as many caramels as Rex, and Lee gets five times as many caramels as Rex. How many does Lee get?

The correct answer is 160. First you need to define your unknowns, or variables. Since the other amounts are stated in terms of the number of caramels Rex gets, let that unknown be r. Then, Drew's caramels would be $4r$ and Lee's would be $5r$. You know that their total is 320. Now set up your equation:

$r + 4r + 5r = 320$ Combine like terms.

$10r = 320$ Divide by 10.

$r = 32$ Rex will get 32 caramels.

Don't grid-in 32 as your answer because the question calls for how many caramels *Lee* will get, which is five times as many: $5 \times 32 = 160$.

You need to keep in mind for what response a problem is actually asking. By the time you have completed several steps or used more than one operation, you may forget the original question.

In just this way, the PSAT has recently become more challenging. It still tests the concepts you learned in arithmetic and elementary algebra and geometry. However, more often than in the past, you are asked to combine multiple skills in order to solve a problem. For example, you might need to use both geometry and a rate formula to compute how fast a certain volume of toothpaste comes out of a dispenser.

EXERCISE

DIRECTIONS: This section consists of student-produced responses, which require you to solve a problem and enter your answer by marking the ovals on the special grids on page 76.

1. If $3^{n+2} = 81$, what does n equal?

2. How many dimes would you pay an ice-cream vendor for twelve 60-cent eskimo pies?

3. This circle graph represents the inventory of Bob's Pet Supplies warehouse. What is the sum of the nonfood items? (Delete the percent sign in your answer.)

Bob's Warehouse Inventory

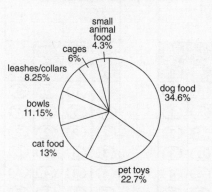

small animal food 4.3%
cages 6%
leashes/collars 8.25%
bowls 11.15%
cat food 13%
pet toys 22.7%
dog food 34.6%

4. What is the mean for Kim, a student who receives 90 in Algebra, 75 in Spanish, 84 in Biology, and 76 in Photography, if the subjects have the following weights: Algebra, 4; Spanish, 3; Biology, 3; and Photography, 1?

5. The quotient of $\sqrt{64} \div (5^2 - 2\sqrt{25})$ is what?

6. A pole that is 20 feet tall casts a shadow that is 12 feet long. At the same time, a tree casts a shadow that is 3 feet long. How tall is the tree?

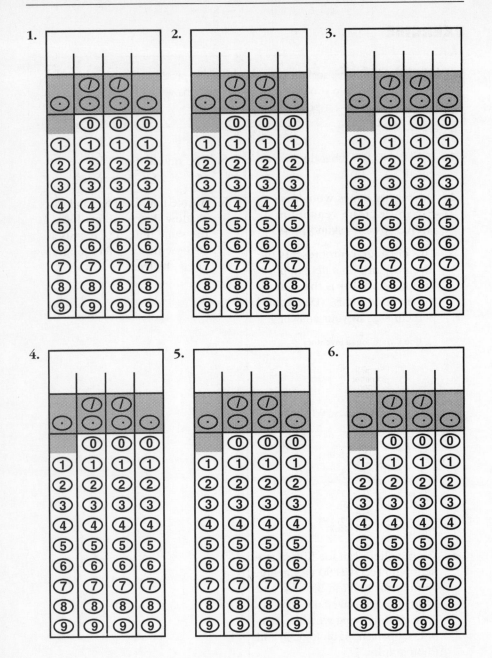

ANSWERS AND EXPLANATIONS

Note: See page 80 for correctly filled in answer grids.

1. **The correct answer is 2.** Since $81 = 3 \times 3 \times 3 \times 3$, then $81 = 3^4$

   $n + 2$ must equal 4
   $n = 2$

   Recall that the superscript numbers, such as the 4 in 3^4, are called *exponents*. Exponents are a kind of shorthand for the number of times you are multiplying a factor by itself. As you saw in this problem, when you multiply two numbers with the same factor or base, you simply add the exponents.

   Watch out! This rule applies to <u>multiplication</u> of the same factor:

   $$3^2 \times 3^4 = 3^{2+4} = 3^6.$$

   It does *not* work for addition: $3^2 + 3^4 \neq 3^6$.

2. **The correct answer is 72.** 12(60 cents) = 720 cents or 72 dimes. Use the power of ten for shortcuts when you can. For example, you could see that 720 was equal to 72×10 or 72 dimes, without actually dividing by ten.

3. **The correct answer is 48.1.**

   Method 1: Add the 4 nonfood items together: $22.7 + 11.15 + 8.25 + 6 = 48.1$

   Method 2: Separate the 3 food items and subtract their sum from 100%: $100 - (34.6 + 13 + 4.3) = 100 - 51.9 = 48.1$

Bob's Warehouse Inventory

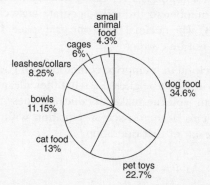

Line graphs, bar graphs, and circle graphs (such as this one) present information in picture form. They usually give an overall view of data, with the opportunity to make comparisons and draw conclusions. A graph may appear in a PSAT problem to test your ability to calculate an answer based on your interpretation of that graph.

4. **The correct answer is 83.** To find the mean (average) of quantities that are weighted, quickly set up a table listing the items, their values, and their weights:

Subject	Value	Weight
Algebra	90	4
Spanish	75	3
Biology	84	3
Photography	76	1

Now multiply the value of each item by its weight and add up these products. Then, divide the sum of the products by the sum of the weights to get Kim's average.

$(90 \times 4) + (75 \times 3) + (84 \times 3) + (76 \times 1) = 360 + 225 + 252 + 76 = 913$

Sum of weights $= 4 + 3 + 3 + 1 = 11$

$913 \div 11 = 83$, Kim's average

5. **The correct answer is $\dfrac{8}{15}$ or .533.** First clear the parentheses:

$$(5^2 - 2\sqrt{25}) = 25 - 2(5) = 15.$$

Next compute the quotient:

$$\sqrt{64} \div 15 = 8 \div 15 = \frac{8}{15} \text{ or } .533.$$

You can write either figure on the grid, but remember to place either the decimal point or the fraction slash in its own column and oval.

Recall that if your solution is a repeating decimal, such as 5.333 . . . , you must round the number to the most accurate answer that will fit in the grid (such as 5.33). The decimal takes one grid space. Less accurate values, such as 5.3, will not be correct.

Also, it may be helpful to memorize common math vocabulary terms, such as *quotient*, so you won't be guessing what they mean on the PSAT. If you don't know a term, you can make an educated guess based on its context within the problem. Here you see an equation with a division sign; the quotient is the result of that operation.

6. **The correct answer is 5.** This is a proportion question. Remember that a proportion describes two ratios that are equal. What ratios are equal in this problem?

$$\frac{\text{the height of the pole}}{\text{the length of the shadow}} = \frac{\text{the height of the tree}}{\text{the length of its shadow}}$$

Now plug in the numbers you know, letting t be the unknown, the height of the tree.

$$\frac{20}{12} = \frac{t}{3} \qquad \text{Cross-multiply.}$$

("The product of the means equals the product of the extremes.")

$$12t = 20 \times 3$$

$$t = \frac{60}{12} = 5 \qquad \text{The tree is 5 feet tall.}$$

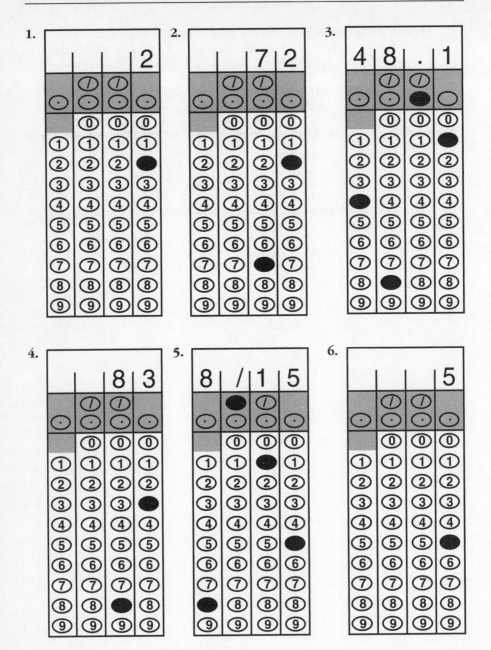

PRACTICE TEST WITH ANSWERS AND EXPLANATIONS

The practice test in this book differs from the actual PSAT in one important way: Each page in the practice test contains no more than two questions, with the answers and explanations immediately following on the next page. This format gives you instant feedback on the answers you selected and immediately clarifies why the correct answer is the best response.

When you take the practice test, try to imitate the actual test as much as possible. Sit at a table or desk in a quiet room free of distractions and work through one full section at a time, as outlined in the study plan on page 8.

Be sure to review all the answer explanations even for the questions you got right. You want to be certain you selected the right response for the right reason.

SECTION 1: CRITICAL READING

DIRECTIONS: Each of the following sentences has one or two blanks, each blank representing a word or words needed to finish the sentence. Each sentence is followed by five words or sets of words marked (A) through (E). From these five choices, pick the one that best completes the meaning of the sentence as a whole.

1. Biologists do not believe that there is a simple, definite dividing line between living and nonliving entities; rather, these entities lie along a/an _____.

   (A) distinction
   (B) boundary
   (C) continuum
   (D) continuation
   (E) affinity

2. Carbon monoxide and volcanic ash are both considered _____ and are equally toxic, in spite of the fact that one is made by human beings and the other is a product of _____.

   (A) contagions . . . earth
   (B) substances . . . God
   (C) irritants . . . industry
   (D) pollutants . . . nature
   (E) concentrations . . . mountains

1. Ⓐ Ⓑ Ⓒ Ⓓ Ⓔ

2. Ⓐ Ⓑ Ⓒ Ⓓ Ⓔ

Answer 1: Ⓒ

This is a sentence of **contrast**—here the word *rather* is the key. The first half of the sentence speaks of a *dividing line*. Now ask yourself, which of the choices contrasts to a dividing line. You can rule out *distinction* and *boundary*, which are the same as a dividing line, so you are left with *continuum, continuation,* and *affinity*. To say "These entities lie along a continuation" makes no sense, nor is it logical to say "These entities lie along an affinity." But to say "These entities lie along a continuum" makes perfect sense.

Answer 2: Ⓓ

This also is a sentence of **contrast**—the phrase *in spite of the fact that* is the key. The sentence is complex and has two blanks, so the first step is to simplify it and look at the first blank:

> Carbon monoxide and volcanic ash are both . . . _____
> and are . . . toxic . . .

Neither *carbon monoxide* nor *volcanic ash* is a *contagion*, so choice (A) is eliminated. Neither *substances* nor *concentrations* are necessarily *toxic*, so you can eliminate choices (B) and (E). You are left with choices (C) (*irritants*, which could conceivably be correct) and (D) (*pollutants*, which could also be correct). Now simplify the second half of the sentence, and look at the second blank:

> One is made by human beings, the other by _____.

The main source of *carbon monoxide* is the motor vehicle, a *human invention. Volcanic ash*, however, is a product, not of *industry*, but of *nature*, the contrasting word.

3. In his poetry we find a
_____ mixture
of images of happiness and
sorrow, images that enhance
the beauty of the work.

   (A) patronizing
   (B) paradoxical
   (C) proprietary
   (D) permeable
   (E) passable

4. Educators find it sad that
today's students are so
_____ about
geography that they actually
believe Puerto Rico is in Africa
and Kenya is in Brazil.

   (A) complacent
   (B) unconventional
   (C) arrogant
   (D) improper
   (E) uninformed

3. (A) (B) (C) (D) (E)

4. (A) (B) (C) (D) (E)

Answer 3: (B)

This is a sentence that shows **cause and effect**. First, simplify the sentence:

> In his poetry we find . . . happiness and sorrow.
> The images of happiness and sorrow enhance beauty.

Because the images enhance *beauty* (or cause it to grow greater), the adjective which describes the images must be positive or at least neutral. This eliminates choices (A), (C) (even if (C) did make sense, which it doesn't), and (E). Choice (D) makes no sense, either. So we are left with the neutral choice, *paradoxical,* choice (B), which is the word for "a contradictory statement" and which therefore best fits in the blank.

Answer 4: (E)

Simplify the sentence and look at it for its total meaning:

> Educators are sad.
> Today's students are (something).
> They believe Puerto Rico is in Africa and Kenya is in Brazil.

The latter two parts of the sentence are connected by the key word *that*, which in this case introduces a causal relationship. Because the students are (something), they believe . . . Now what state of affairs would best describe people who believe Puerto Rico is in Africa? People can't be said to be improper (although their behavior might be), so choice (D) can be eliminated right away. The people in the sentence *might* be complacent, unconventional, or arrogant; however, we can't be sure. Given the erroneous way they would probably answer questions, they are certainly *uninformed*, though, so that is the best answer.

5. Her harsh
   _____ often
   left us in tears, so that we
   would go home
   _____.

   (A) compliments . . . deter-
   mined
   (B) criticism . . . devastated
   (C) frustration . . . placid
   (D) oratory . . . indecisive
   (E) remonstrance . . . ebullient

6. The Galapagos Islands form a
   lonely archipelago, completely
   _____ far out
   in the Pacific Ocean, 600 miles
   from the mainland.

   (A) isolated
   (B) consummated
   (C) preoccupied
   (D) erected
   (E) suspended

---

5. Ⓐ Ⓑ Ⓒ Ⓓ Ⓔ

6. Ⓐ Ⓑ Ⓒ Ⓓ Ⓔ

Answer 5:   (B)

This is a **cause-and-effect** sentence. Begin by looking at the word that is described by the adjective *harsh*. It must be a negative word; something harsh is very often something that has a negative effect. Compliments hardly ever cause hurt, and frustration can't be harsh, so choices (A) and (C) are immediately eliminated. Criticism, oratory (of a certain kind), and remonstrance *can* all cause hurt, so you must look even more closely. The key words *so that* indicate causality—the negative word in the first blank causes whatever is in the second blank. To be *ebullient* is to be lively and enthusiastic, so you can scratch choice (E). Something negative *can* cause *indecisiveness*, but it's more likely to cause *devastation*, so choice (B) is the best answer.

Answer 6:   (A)

This is a **definition** sentence. Begin by simplifying:

> The Galapagos are lonely.
> The Galapagos are far out in the Pacific Ocean.

Choices (B), (C), and (D) can be eliminated immediately. *Consummated* and *preoccupied* simply don't describe islands. It is also doubtful an island has been *erected*—generally, islands arise naturally. Now look at the overall meaning of the sentence. The islands are *lonely* and *far* out from the mainland. Which of the remaining two choices best describes a lonely, far-off place? Common sense and logic will tell you that *isolated* fits the bill best.

DIRECTIONS: The passages below are followed by questions based on their content. (The first two passages are related and some of the questions that follow them are based on that relationship.) Answer the questions on the basis of what is *stated* or *implied* in each passage.

Questions 7–13 are based on the following passages.

Passage 1

This passage is an excerpt from H. G. Wells' novel, The Time Machine.

Line   The thing the Time Traveler held in his hand was a glittering metallic framework, scarcely larger than a small clock, and very delicately made. There was ivory in it, and some transparent crystalline substance . . .

The Medical Man got up out of his chair and peered into the thing.
5   "It's beautifully made," he said.

"It took two years to make," retorted the Time Traveler. . . . "Presently I am going to press the lever, and off the machine will go. It will vanish, pass into future Time, and disappear. Have a good look at the thing. Look at the table, too, and satisfy yourselves there is no trickery."
10   . . . We all saw the lever turn. I am absolutely certain there was no trickery. There was a breath of wind, and the lamp flame jumped. One of the candles on the mantel was blown out, and the little machine suddenly swung round, became indistinct, was seen as a ghost for a second perhaps, as an eddy of faintly glittering brass and ivory; and it was gone—vanished!
15   Save for the lamp the table was bare.

. . . We stared at each other. . . .

. . . "You mean to say that that machine has traveled into the future?" said Filby.

"Into the future or the past—I don't, for certain, know which."
20   After an interval the Psychologist had an inspiration. "It must have gone into the past if it has gone anywhere," he said.

"Why?" said the Time Traveler.

"Because I presume that it has not moved in space, and if it traveled into the future it would still be here all this time, since it must have
25   traveled through this time."

"But," I said, "If it traveled into the past it would have been visible when we came first into this room; and last Thursday when we were here; and the Thursday before that; and so forth!"

"Serious objections," remarked the Provincial Mayor, with an air of
30   impartiality, turning towards the Time Traveler.

"Not a bit," said the Time Traveler, and, to the Psychologist: "You think. You can explain that. It's presentation below the threshold, you know, diluted presentation."

"Of course," said the Psychologist, and reassured us. "That's a simple
35   point of psychology. I should have thought of it. It's plain enough, and
helps the paradox delightfully. We cannot see it, nor can we appreciate
this machine, any more than we can the spoke of a wheel spinning, or a
bullet flying through the air. If it is traveling through time fifty times or a
hundred times faster than we are, if it gets through a minute while we get
40   through a second, the impression it creates will of course be only
one-fiftieth or one-hundredth of what it would make if it were not
traveling in time. That's plain enough." He passed his hand through the
space in which the machine had been. "You see?" he said, laughing.

Passage 2

This passage is based on A Brief History of Time *by Stephen Hawking.*

In his best-selling book *A Brief History of Time*, Stephen Hawking
45   states that, although the laws of science do not distinguish between the
forward and backward directions of time, time travel for human beings is
nonetheless not possible. For one thing, the second law of thermodynamics holds that in a closed system such as our universe, disorder always
increases with time. A cup that falls from the table and shatters will not
50   reassemble—or re-order—itself and jump back onto the table. For another
thing, psychologically, we remember the past, but we do not remember
the future. These processes are called "arrows of time," and they travel in
the same direction, from past to future.

There is also a third "arrow of time," the cosmological arrow of time,
55   in which the universe expands, rather than contracts. The cosmological
arrow of time, however, may not always travel in this one direction. The
universe may someday reach the end of expansion, at which point
disorder will be nearly absolute and therefore will not be able to increase.
Then the universe may start to contract again. This is no help for would-be
60   human time travelers, however. In order to invent theories of expanding
and contracting universes, in order to even contemplate inventing a time
machine, we must think and learn and thus increase the order of our own
brains. As Hawking explains, we do this by consuming food—an ordered
form of energy—and converting it to heat—a disordered form of energy.
65   In a universe in which disorder could not increase, we could not exist.

A special case in which the descent from order to disorder might be
reversed is inside a black hole. And so it could be supposed, Hawking says,
that an astronaut falling into a black hole would theoretically be able to
remember the future. This would not happen in actuality, however,
70   because the astronaut would be torn apart, or as Hawking puts it, "turned
to spaghetti."

7. Based solely on the passages, if Stephen Hawking and the Time Traveler met and discussed the topic of time travel, they would be most likely to agree that
   - (A) we remember the past but not the future.
   - (B) the second law of thermo-dynamics would make time travel difficult.
   - (C) a contracting universe would be of no help to time travelers.
   - (D) everything in the universe tends toward disorder.
   - (E) the laws of science do not distinguish between the forward and backward directions of time.

8. The main point of Passage 2 is that Stephen Hawking believes that
   - (A) time travel is not possible for human beings.
   - (B) a disordered universe cannot re-order itself.
   - (C) human beings need disorder to live.
   - (D) order may actually increase in a black hole.
   - (E) the cosmological arrow of time may fly toward the past.

7. Ⓐ Ⓑ Ⓒ Ⓓ Ⓔ

8. Ⓐ Ⓑ Ⓒ Ⓓ Ⓔ

Answer 7: Ⓔ

The Time Traveler claims to have demonstrated time travel, so he must believe that the laws of science do not distinguish between the forward and backward directions of time. The first sentence of Passage 2 states that Stephen Hawking believes the same thing.

Answer 8: Ⓐ

This point is made at the beginning of paragraph 1. All the other choices are used to support it but are too narrow to be the main argument.

9. To which of the following objects in Passage 1 is the time machine in motion compared?

   (A) A glittering metallic framework (lines 1–2)
   (B) A breath of wind (line 11)
   (C) A lamp flame (line 11)
   (D) A paradox (line 36)
   (E) The spoke of a wheel spinning (line 37)

10. Which of the following beliefs would the Time Traveler likely hold regarding Hawking's concept of the "arrows of time?"

    (A) The concept is correct only with regard to the cosmological arrow.
    (B) The concept is correct except in the case of the cosmological arrow.
    (C) The arrows might some-how damage the time machine.
    (D) The arrows might fly in a reverse direction in a black hole.
    (E) The arrows increase the disorder of the universe.

9. Ⓐ Ⓑ Ⓒ Ⓓ Ⓔ

10. Ⓐ Ⓑ Ⓒ Ⓓ Ⓔ

Answer 9:   (E)

The key word in the question is *compared*; the words to look at in the passage are *any more than*. In the final paragraph, the narrator of the story says that the time machine in motion cannot be seen *any more than the spoke of a wheel spinning*, which implies a comparison. Choice (A) expresses what the time machine *is made of* and choices (B) and (C) what the time machine *causes*. Choice (D) refers to the time machine's *ability* to travel past the point where the people in the story are standing without its being seen, which is a *paradox*.

Answer 10:   (A)

According to Hawking, it might be possible for the *cosmological arrow* of time to fly toward both past and future, which would be necessary for time travel (which the Time Traveler obviously believes in) to occur. To believe in choice (B) would be to believe that time travel is not possible, because the other arrows Hawking refers to can travel in only one direction. Choice (C) makes no sense—Hawking's arrows are not real, physical arrows. There is no indication in Passage 1 that the Time Traveler is aware of either choices (D) or (E).

11. When Stephen Hawking says that, in our universe, "[a] cup that falls from the table and shatters will not reassemble—or re-order—itself and jump back onto the table" (lines 49–50), the point he is trying to illustrate is that

    (A) our universe is a closed system.

    (B) we remember the past but not the future.

    (C) our universe is a place of ever-growing disorder.

    (D) the expanding universe may someday start to contract.

    (E) the laws of science are irrefutable.

12. What does the Time Traveler mean in lines 32 and 33 when he tells the Psychologist, "It's presentation below the threshold . . ."?

    (A) It's impossible to tell whether the time machine is traveling to the past or to the future.

    (B) The time machine has not moved in space.

    (C) The time machine can no longer be "appreciated" (that is, seen) because it is no longer in the room with them.

    (D) The time machine is traveling too fast through time to be seen.

    (E) The time machine is no longer moving through time.

11. (A) (B) (C) (D) (E)

12. (A) (B) (C) (D) (E)

Answer 11: Ⓒ

Approach this question by looking at the ideas expressed near the quoted statement. Immediately before the quote, the passage states Hawking's idea that *in a closed system such as our universe, disorder always increases with time*. The passage assumes *our universe is a closed system,* choice (A), but does not attempt to illustrate the fact. Neither the fact that *we remember the past but not the future,* choice (B), nor the fact that *the expanding universe may someday start to contract,* choice (D), has anything to do with the cup's falling and shattering. Nowhere in the passage does it mention that Hawking believes *the laws of science are irrefutable*.

Answer 12: Ⓓ

Again, look at the ideas expressed immediately around the quoted statement. In the very next paragraph, the Psychologist suddenly understands what the Time Traveler meant by the statement and restates the statement by saying "Of course. . . . We cannot see it, nor can we appreciate this machine, any more than we can the spoke of a wheel spinning. . . ." meaning that it is traveling too fast. Choices (A) and (B) are true but have nothing to do with the fact that the time machine cannot be seen. Choices (C) and (E) are false—the people in the story assume the time machine is in the room with them and that it is moving through time.

13. Which of the following would Stephen Hawking say is the main thing that would keep the Time Traveler's machine from actually working?

(A) The laws of science

(B) The second law of thermodynamics

(C) Remembering the past and predicting the future

(D) The cosmological arrow of time

(E) Encounter with a black hole

13. Ⓐ Ⓑ Ⓒ Ⓓ Ⓔ

Answer 13: (B)

It is directly stated in paragraph 1. All other things being equal, choices (A), (D), and (E) might actually support the idea that time travel *is* possible. Choice (C) is incorrect because nowhere in the passage does it say that we can predict the future.

Questions 14–19 are based on the following passage.

Line   Lucid dreaming is dreaming and being aware that you are dreaming. It
occurs during the rapid-eye-movement (REM) phase of sleep. The word
"lucid" refers to a sense of mental clarity. In the midst of a dream, the
dreamer realizes—usually slowly, as a result of some incongruous
5   element—that what is happening is happening in a dream. Reports of
lucid dreaming go back to ancient times—Aristotle mentioned it in the
fourth century B.C., as did St. Augustine in the year 415 A.D. Most people
have had at least one lucid dream.

The dream of flying without an airplane is fairly common and for
10   many people is a magical experience. They can levitate or actually fly, soar
over forests and streams or near the ceilings of large auditoriums, knowing
all the while that they cannot fall because they are dreaming. Or perhaps
the dreamer has a romance with an unattainable or forbidden person, with
the knowledge that there will be no social repercussions. Lucid dreaming
15   opens up realms of adventure and fantasy that otherwise exist only in films
and stories. Some people say they can actually prolong their lucid dreams
through an act of will.

Some claim that they have learned how to have such dreams, that
they have mastered the art of lucid dreaming and that it regularly helps
20   them reach their goals. They say that they are able to manipulate the
dream-state so as to prepare for a physical or mental challenge, that they
can problem-solve by trying out new behaviors in the safe dream
environment. Some think that lucid dreaming can speed physical healing.
And some claim to have had mystical experiences in lucid dreams, to have
25   felt a wonderful sense of wholeness, of oneness with God or with the rest
of the universe. Such dreams are often characterized by vivid color or soft,
bright light.

Unfortunately, for some people, being lucid in a dream is not
accompanied by a feeling of control. There are therapists, however, who
30   believe that a sense of control can be learned and that, for people plagued
by nightmares, lucid dreaming may provide valuable therapy and insight to
help them overcome the terror. If one knows one is dreaming, one knows
that nothing in the dream can hurt one. The fear is all too real, but there is
a way to face and overcome it that involves no physical threat. With
35   practice, these therapists say, the dreamer can master the art of controlling
the dream and can transform a feared person or thing into something
benign—a beast into a beautiful human being, say, as might happen in a
fairy tale. Monsters may become friends when confronted in lucid dreams,
and consequently the dreamer will feel stronger, more empowered, in
waking life.

14. Which of the following best expresses the main idea of the passage?

   (A) Lucid dreaming is usually a positive experience and is sometimes even therapeutic.

   (B) Lucid dreaming imparts a sense of wonder that can seem mystical.

   (C) Lucid dreaming has been reported as far back as Aristotle and St. Augustine.

   (D) Lucid dreaming can be either a wonderfully positive or nightmarishly negative experience.

   (E) Lucid dreaming invariably leads to a sense of strength and empowerment.

15. The author uses the examples of flying and forbidden romance (paragraph 2) to illustrate that lucid dreaming

   (A) can be therapeutic.

   (B) can be frightening.

   (C) can be magical.

   (D) is fairly common.

   (E) is an age-old phenomenon.

14. (A) (B) (C) (D) (E)

15. (A) (B) (C) (D) (E)

Answer 14: (A)

Although the author frequently uses the phrase *some think* or *some claim,* there is no indication that he or she disagrees with choice (A), and this choice, unlike choices (B) and (C), is broad enough to be the main point. The passage describes lucid dreaming as mostly positive and ends with a long paragraph on the therapeutic effects of lucid dreaming. The best overall approach to this problem is to first weed out the choices that contradict what is in the passage. Regarding choice (D), the author does state that lucid dreaming can include nightmares but maintains that even the experience of lucid nightmares can have a positive outcome. Regarding choice (E), the author implies that lucid dreaming may lead to a sense of empowerment but does not say that this is invariable. As noted above, choices (B) and (C) are in the passage, but both are too narrow to be the main point.

Answer 15: (C)

Approach the question by first looking at the ideas expressed very near the examples of *flying* and *forbidden romance*. The examples are given in lines 10–14, immediately after the statement that lucid dreaming can be *magical*. The other choices are in other paragraphs and relate to discussions of different matters.

16. Which of the following elements of the passage best demonstrates the therapeutic value of lucid dreams?

   (A) The mention in paragraph 1 of Aristotle and St. Augustine

   (B) The mention in paragraph 2 that some people claim they can prolong their lucid dreams

   (C) The mention in paragraph 3 that some dreamers claim to have had mystical experiences in lucid dreams

   (D) The mention in paragraph 3 that lucid dreams are often accompanied by color and light

   (E) The mention in paragraph 4 that monsters may become friends in lucid dreams

17. In the context of paragraph 3, the word *mystical* (line 24) most nearly means

   (A) puzzling.
   (B) imaginary.
   (C) spiritual.
   (D) mysterious.
   (E) enchanted.

---

16. (A) (B) (C) (D) (E)

17. (A) (B) (C) (D) (E)

Answer 16: (E)

Look closely at the discussion that surrounds the mention of therapeutic value in paragraph 4—therapeutic value is talked about specifically in connection with turning dream-monsters into friends. Mystical experiences and color and light in dreams, choices (C) and (D), may be therapeutic, but they are not pointed out in the passage. Choices (A) and (B) are not specifically related to the therapeutic value of lucid dreams anywhere in the passage.

Answer 17: (C)

Again, examine the discussion surrounding the word *mystical*. Although choices (A), (B), (D), and (E) could possibly be qualities of a mystical experience, only *oneness with God and the rest of the universe* is specifically mentioned in paragraph 3 in connection with the word *mystical*.

18. In the context of paragraph 4, the reference to a *fairy tale* (line 38) is most closely related to which of the following processes that sometimes take place in lucid dreams?

    (A) Transformation
    (B) Control
    (C) Empowerment
    (D) Confrontation
    (E) Learning

19. In terms of the main point of the essay, the mention of Aristotle and St. Augustine in lines 6-7 can best be characterized as

    (A) a concrete example essential to the main point.
    (B) an aside with only marginal bearing on the main point.
    (C) a definition to help the reader understand the main point.
    (D) a hint that the main point is still under debate.
    (E) a formal introduction to the main point.

---

18. (A) (B) (C) (D) (E)

19. (A) (B) (C) (D) (E)

Answer 18: (A)

Use the same approach to this question as that suggested for question 24. In paragraph 4, the author specifically states that, in a lucid dream, a transformation may occur *as in a fairy tale*. Choices (B) through (E) are all mentioned in the passage as happening in lucid dreams but not in such specific connection with a fairy tale.

Answer 19: (B)

There is only one mention of Aristotle and St. Augustine in the whole passage, and it is unrelated to any of the other choices. It can only be regarded as an interesting aside.

Questions 20–21 are based on the following passage.

The following excerpt is from an address by Senator Hillary Rodham Clinton, "New American Strategies for Security and Peace," *at the Center for American Progress on October 29, 2003.*

Line Of course in a democracy, there always is tension between the
information that the Executive Branch needs to keep secret and the
information that must be provided to the public to have an informed
citizenry. There are no easy answers to striking the right balance. But we
5   must always be vigilant against letting our desire to keep information
confidential be used as a pretext for classifying information that is more
about political embarrassment than national security. Let me be absolutely
clear. This is not a propensity that is confined to one party or the other. It
is a propensity of power that we must guard against.

20. The main purpose of Clinton's address is to advocate an end to

   (A) tension between the Executive Branch and the public.

   (B) secrets kept by the Executive Branch solely for political reasons.

   (C) witholding of information by the political party to which Clinton is opposed.

   (D) public insistance on the release of classified information.

   (E) false information released by the Executive branch.

21. A main implication of the passage is that, with information, comes

   (A) power.

   (B) wisdom.

   (C) security.

   (D) deceit.

   (E) confusion.

20. (A) (B) (C) (D) (E)

21. (A) (B) (C) (D) (E)

Answer 20: Ⓑ

Choice (C) is contradicted by the passage, when Clinton says *This [withholding information] is not a propensity that is confined to one party or the other.* Choices (A), (D), and (E) are not supported by the passage.

Answer 21: Ⓐ

Although choice (C) is mentioned in the text, Clinton says security may be used as a pretext for withholding information—not that security comes with information. Choices (B), (D), and (E) may be true, but they are not implied by the passage.

Questions 22–23 are based on the following passage.

The following exerpt is from the U.S. Department of Energy archives.

Line [In 1929, Ernest] Lawrence invented a unique circular particle accelerator,
which he referred to as his "proton merry-go-round," but which became
better known as the cyclotron. The first cyclotron was a pie-shaped
concoction of glass, sealing wax, and bronze. A kitchen chair and a
5   wire-coiled clothes tree were also enlisted to make the device work.
Despite its Rube Goldberg appearance, the cyclotron proved Lawrence's
point: whirling particles around to boost their energies, then casting them
toward a target like stones from a slingshot is the most efficient and
effective way to smash open atomic nuclei.

22. In the context of the passage, the phrase "Rube Goldberg" most likely means

(A) impractical.

(B) sophisticated.

(C) technical.

(D) ingenious.

(E) inconspicuous.

23. The colloquial phrase "proton merry-go-round" primarily serves to make the passage more accessible to readers who

(A) are uninterested in technolgy.

(B) lack technical expertise.

(C) plan to become scientists.

(D) understand complex metaphors.

(E) believe technology is dangerous.

22. (A) (B) (C) (D) (E)

23. (A) (B) (C) (D) (E)

Answer 22: (A)

It would not make sense to say that the cyclotron was effective despite appearing *sophisticated*, *technical*, or *ingenious*—choices (B), (C), and (D). Choice (E) is incorrect because the device is described in a way that makes it seem outlandish in appearance, and therefore conspicuous.

Answer 23: (B)

The passage says that whirling atoms and then casting them at a target is an effective way to *smash open atomic nuclei*. The other choices are not reflected in the passage.

Questions 24–25 are based on the following passage.

This excerpt is from Jules Verne's Around the World in 80 Days.

Line Was Phileas Fogg rich? Undoubtedly. But those who knew him best could
not imagine how he had made his fortune, and Mr. Fogg was the last
person to whom to apply for the information. He was not lavish, nor, on
the contrary, avaricious; for, whenever he knew that money was needed
5   for a noble, useful, or benevolent purpose, he supplied it quietly and
sometimes anonymously. He was, in short, the least communicative of
men. He talked very little, and seemed all the more mysterious for his
taciturn manner. His daily habits were quite open to observation; but
whatever he did was so exactly the same thing that he had always done
10   before, that the wits of the curious were fairly puzzled.

24. The main purpose of the
question that opens the passage
is to

(A) inform the reader.
(B) goad the reader.
(C) test the reader.
(D) intrigue the reader.
(E) disturb the reader.

25. In the context of the passage,
which is the best meaning of
the word "avaricious" (line 4)?

(A) Bitter
(B) Cruel
(C) Greedy
(D) Dishonest
(E) Ignorant

24. Ⓐ Ⓑ Ⓒ Ⓓ Ⓔ

25. Ⓐ Ⓑ Ⓒ Ⓓ Ⓔ

Answer 24: (D)

The question has the effect of making the reader want to know the answer. Choice (A) is wrong because the question has no information in it. Choices (B) and (E) are wrong because there is nothing unpleasant in the question that would *goad* or *disturb* the reader. Choice (C) is wrong because the question is rhetorical, and therefore not meant to be answered by the reader.

Answer 25: (C)

The passage says that Phileas Fogg was <u>not</u> *avaricious*; this is followed by the suggestion that he was often generous. The other choices are not supported by the passage.

DIRECTIONS: This section consists of multiple-choice problems, each of which has five possible answers. Solve each problem. Then decide which is the best of the choices given and fill in the corresponding oval.

1. If $6(m + 2) = 24$, which of the following is true?

   (A) $m + 2 = 18$
   (B) $m + 12 = 24$
   (C) $6m + 2 = 24$
   (D) $6m + 12 = 144$
   (E) $6m + 12 = 24$

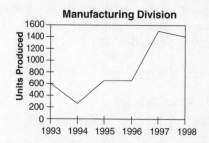

Manufacturing Division

2. According to the graph, between what years did the Manufacturing Division show the sharpest rise in production?

   (A) 1993 to 1994
   (B) 1994 to 1995
   (C) 1995 to 1996
   (D) 1996 to 1997
   (E) 1997 to 1998

1. Ⓐ Ⓑ Ⓒ Ⓓ Ⓔ

2. Ⓐ Ⓑ Ⓒ Ⓓ Ⓔ

Answer 1:   (E)

Concepts: • Functions
            • Solving equations

$$6(m + 2) = 24$$
$$6m + 6(2) = 24$$
$$6m + 12 = 24$$

Use the distributive property of algebra, $a(b + c) = ab + ac$, to simplify the left side of the equation to $6m + 6(2)$. Carry out the multiplication of 6 times 2 to arrive at $6m + 12 = 24$, which is the right answer, choice (E). The other four choices do not apply the distributive property correctly. Note that this equation can be further simplified to $6m = 12$ and $m = 2$, but these answers are not among your choices.

Answer 2:   (D)

Concept: • Tables and graphs

Choices (A) and (E) each show a drop in production. Choice (C) shows no change. In choice (B), there is a slight rise in production. Choice (D) shows a sharp rise.

Remember, a line graph is a pictorial representation that shows trends or continuity. You need to quickly understand a graph's parts to interpret the data it represents. To do this, be sure to read the title and labels on each axis of the graph.

The change in production is the vertical distance between years. By merely looking at the graph, you should be able to see that the sharpest rise in production is between the years 1996 and 1997. It represents about 1½ times the other rise in production, choice (B). Notice you do not have to compute the actual changes in units produced to answer the problem.

3. How much is $\frac{1}{4}$ of $\frac{n}{4}$?

(A) $\frac{1}{n}$

(B) n

(C) $\frac{n}{16}$

(D) $\frac{1}{16}$

(E) $16n$

4. A 32-year-old woman has a 2-year-old niece. In how many years will the woman be 4 times as old as her niece?

(A) 8

(B) 10

(C) $4x$

(D) $2 + x$

(E) 16

3. (A) (B) (C) (D) (E)

4. (A) (B) (C) (D) (E)

Answer 3:   Ⓒ

Concepts: • Fractions
                 • Arithmetic

The word "of" is often used to mean "multiply." In this problem, multiply the numerators together, then the denominators, to get choice (C):

$$\frac{1}{4} \times \frac{n}{4} = \frac{n}{16}$$

Choice (A) takes the reciprocal of the second fraction and multiplies, while choice (B) takes the reciprocal of the first fraction and multiplies. Choice (D) forgets the variable n altogether or mistakenly divides it out. Choice (E) multiplies $1 \times 4 \times n \times 4$.

Answer 4:   Ⓐ

Concepts: • Word problems
                 • Solving equations

Let x equal the time in years it takes to reach the age ratio of 4 to 1. At that time, x years in the future, the niece will be $2 + x$ years old, and her aunt will be $32 + x$ years old. Set up an equation to satisfy the ratio of ages as 4 to 1:

$$4(2 + x) = 32 + x$$
$$8 + 4x = 32 + x$$
$$3x = 24$$
$$x = 8$$

Check out the answer by substituting: In 8 years, the aunt will be 40 years old, and her niece will be 10. The aunt will then be 4 times as old as her niece.

When solving problems by equation, read carefully to determine which element should be the variable, the unknown quantity. Determine a relationship that may be written as an equation, solve it, and check the answer by substitution.

5. If $.3^2 = \sqrt{y}$, then $y =$

   (A) .3

   (B) .03

   (C) .09

   (D) .081

   (E) .0081

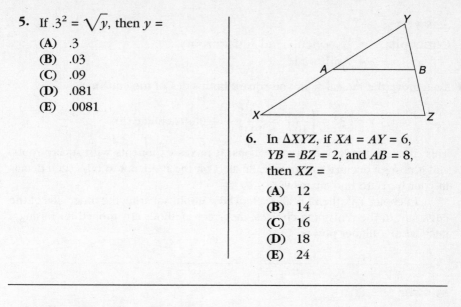

6. In $\triangle XYZ$, if $XA = AY = 6$, $YB = BZ = 2$, and $AB = 8$, then $XZ =$

   (A) 12

   (B) 14

   (C) 16

   (D) 18

   (E) 24

5. (A) (B) (C) (D) (E)

6. (A) (B) (C) (D) (E)

Answer 5: (E)

Concepts: • Exponents and square roots
• Arithmetic

To remove the radical sign, you square both sides of the equation.

$$y = (.3^2)^2 = .3^4 = \left(\frac{3}{10}\right)^4 = \frac{81}{10,000} = .0081, \text{ choice (E)}.$$

This problem is tricky for two reasons. It mixes exponents with square roots, and it raises a decimal to a power. Be alert on the PSAT not to miss such details in your hurry to find an answer.

In choice (A), the radical is removed without squaring the other side of the equation. In the remaining choices, incorrect methods are applied for raising a decimal to a higher power.

Answer 6: (C)

Concept: • Geometry

Remember that the line that joins two midpoints of two sides of a triangle will be parallel to the third side and equal to one half of that side. Because $XA = AY$ and $YB = BZ$, points A and B are the midpoints of their sides. Then, the line that joins them, AB, is parallel to XZ and is half its length. So, if $AB = 8$, XZ will be twice that, or 16. All other choices arrive at false answers.

Another approach is to note that $\triangle YAB \sim \triangle YXZ$, since they have a common angle, Y, and the two included sides are proportional $\left(\frac{1}{2} \text{ of the longer sides}\right)$.

Therefore, $\frac{DE}{AC} = \frac{1}{2}$ or, in this problem, $\frac{8}{16}$.

7. A man completes $\frac{2}{5}$ of his chores in an hour. If he works at the same rate, how many additional hours will it take for him to complete his chores?

   (A) $\frac{3}{5}$
   (B) 0.5
   (C) 1.5
   (D) 2.5
   (E) 90

8. A cake serves 9 people. How many cakes will be needed to serve a party of 196 people?

   (A) 21
   (B) 22
   (C) 23
   (D) 24
   (E) 25

7. Ⓐ Ⓑ Ⓒ Ⓓ Ⓔ

8. Ⓐ Ⓑ Ⓒ Ⓓ Ⓔ

Answer 7:   Ⓒ

Concepts: • Fractions
             • Direct proportions

This question, like many on the PSAT, can be approached from more than one angle. You could set up the problem as a direct proportion. The more the man works, the more he completes of his chores, so let x = the time required to finish his chores.

$$\frac{\text{part of work done}}{\text{time (in hours)}} = \frac{\frac{2}{5}}{1} = \frac{1}{x}$$

Cross-multiply, to get $\frac{2}{5}x = 1$

$$x = \frac{5}{2} = 2\frac{1}{2} = 2.5$$

Be careful! The answer to the equation is 2.5 hours, choice (D). But since the man has already worked for 1 hour, he has only 1.5 hours more to work, so the correct answer is choice (C). Choice (E) solves the problem in terms of minutes (1.5 hours = 90 minutes), but the question asks for the answer in hours. Choice (A) answers what fraction to add to $\frac{2}{5}$ to make a whole (completed chores), but it does not answer the number of hours needed.

Another way to approach this problem is to use mental math. If $\frac{2}{5}$ of the man's chores are completed in an hour, then another $\frac{2}{5}$ will be completed in a second hour. There remains $\frac{1}{5}$ of his chores to finish, which will take half the time it takes to complete $\frac{2}{5}$ of the chores, or .5 hours. So, 1 hour + 1 hour + .5 hours = 2.5 hours.

Answer 8:   Ⓑ

Concepts: • Arithmetic
             • Rounding

$196 \div 9 = 21.7 = 21\frac{7}{10}$. Since you would not purchase part of a cake, you round up the answer to 22 cakes, choice (B). Choice (A)'s answer of 21 cakes wouldn't serve everyone, and the remaining choices suggest too many cakes.

9. Four straight lines lie in the same plane, intersecting each other at point A. What is the sum of the measures of the nonoverlapping angles?

   (A) 60°
   (B) 90°
   (C) 180°
   (D) 360°
   (E) 380°

The difference between three times the number a and 5 is 73.

10. Which of the following equations could be used to express the relationship in the above statement?

   (A) $3a + 5 = 73$
   (B) $3a - 5 = 73$
   (C) $3(a - 5) = 73$
   (D) $a - 2(5) = 73$
   (E) $a - 3 + 5 = 73$

---

9. Ⓐ Ⓑ Ⓒ Ⓓ Ⓔ

10. Ⓐ Ⓑ Ⓒ Ⓓ Ⓔ

Answer 9:   (D)

Concept: • Geometry

The nonoverlapping angles formed at the intersection point of four straight lines add up to one circle, or choice (D), 360°. The strategy of sketching a problem can help you visualize the situation presented. No matter how you draw the four lines, if they meet the stated requirements, the sum of the measures of their angles is the sum of the angles that make up a circle.

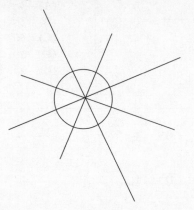

From your sketch, you can infer the meaning of *nonoverlapping*. The problem is telling you: "Don't count angles more than once by combining them into a larger angle."

Answer 10:   (B)

Concepts: • Word problems
　　　　　　　 • Arithmetic functions

Translating words into algebraic expressions takes practice. Look for word clues. In this example, start with the most straightforward part, "is 73," which becomes the right side of the equation, "= 73." The left side of the equation describes subtraction (the difference) between two quantities, $3a$ (three times a) and 5. Translating the sentence one step at a time like this, you arrive at choice (B), $3a - 5 = 73$.

If you picked choice (A), you added instead of subtracting. Choices (C), (D), and (E) are wrong because they misinterpret the math terms given.

11. A fertilizer contains 78% carbon compounds, and the rest is ammonia. If 80% of the ammonia contains the chemical element nitrogen, what percent of this fertilizer is nitrogen?

(A) 17.6%
(B) 22%
(C) 26%
(D) 62.4%
(E) 78%

12. Raffle tickets numbered from 1 to 60, inclusive, are placed in a hat. One ticket is to be selected at random. What is the probability that the selected raffle ticket will have a single-digit number on it?

(A) $\dfrac{1}{60}$

(B) $\dfrac{9}{60}$

(C) $\dfrac{9}{58}$

(D) $\dfrac{1}{6}$

(E) $\dfrac{59}{60}$

11. (A) (B) (C) (D) (E)

12. (A) (B) (C) (D) (E)

Answer 11: Ⓐ

Concepts: • Percentages
• Mental math

This question seems complicated, but one easy subtraction is all that is necessary when you visualize the problem.

Mentally calculate what part of the fertilizer is ammonia: 100% − 78% (carbon compounds) = 22%. Just a part of this ammonia (80%) contains nitrogen. Therefore, the correct answer *has to be less than 22%*, which is the entire amount of ammonia in the fertilizer. Note that only one answer choice is less than 22%. The only possible answer is 17.6%, choice (A). To help you visualize a problem on the PSAT, you can make a sketch:

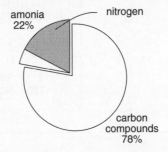

You can also calculate the exact answer as follows: 80% of (100% − 78%) = 80% × 22% = .8(22%) = 17.6%. However, using common sense, you can solve this problem without time-consuming calculations.

Answer 12: Ⓑ

Concept: • Probability

There are nine single-digit numbers (1, 2, 3, 4, 5, 6, 7, 8, and 9) in the series 1 through 60, inclusive. Since there is a total of 60 raffle tickets in the hat, there are 9 chances out of 60, or a probability of $\frac{9}{60}$, choice (B), that the ticket selected will have a single-digit number on it.

Choice (C) does not take into account the word "inclusive." Choice (D) assumes there are 10 single-digit numbers in the series.

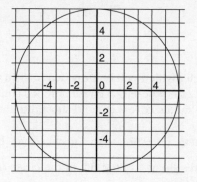

13. What is the circumference of the circle in the figure above?

(A) 6π

(B) 12π

(C) $\dfrac{36}{2}\pi$

(D) 24π

(E) 36π

14. When $xy = 24$, what is the value of the ratio of x to y?

(A) 1 to 24

(B) 4 to 6

(C) 6 to 4

(D) 24 to 1

(E) It cannot be determined from the information given.

13. Ⓐ Ⓑ Ⓒ Ⓓ Ⓔ

14. Ⓐ Ⓑ Ⓒ Ⓓ Ⓔ

Answer 13: Ⓑ

Concepts: • Circle geometry
               • Coordinate geometry

The formula for the circumference of a circle, which will be provided for you at the beginning of each math section, is $C = 2\pi r$, where C = circumference and r = radius. Count the number of squares the radius covers (6) and substitute into the formula: $C = 2\pi(6) = 12\pi$.

Another strategy is to eyeball the figure and estimate the answer. Start by counting the approximate number of squares along $\frac{1}{4}$ of the rim of the circle (in one quadrant of the graph). There are about 8. Multiply by 4 quadrants, $8 \times 4 = 32$. The answer must be close to 32.

Then, evaluate the answer choices using 3.14 or 3 for π. Only choice (B) or 12π is close to 32.

Answer 14: Ⓔ

Concepts: • Ratios
               • Variables

Some PSAT items will test whether you can recognize that there are not enough data to answer the question. In this problem, there is not enough information to evaluate the ratio of x to y. We need to know not only the product but also one of the variables in order to write the ratio.

For example, if $x = 3$, you can substitute to find that $y = 8$. The value of the ratio of x to y would then be 3 to 8.

Remember, a ratio is an expression that compares two quantities. It can be written one of three ways:

$$3 \text{ to } 8 \text{ or } 3{:}8 \text{ or } \frac{3}{8}$$

15. If $n > 1$, which of the following expressions decrease(s) in value as n increases?

    I. $n^2 - 3n$

    II. $n + \dfrac{1}{n}$

    III. $\dfrac{1}{n + 1}$

  (A) I only

  (B) II only

  (C) III only

  (D) I and II only

  (E) I, II, and III

16. If the width and length of a rectangle are doubled, by what percent is the area increased?

  (A) 30%

  (B) 100%

  (C) 200%

  (D) 300%

  (E) 400%

---

15. Ⓐ Ⓑ Ⓒ Ⓓ Ⓔ

16. Ⓐ Ⓑ Ⓒ Ⓓ Ⓔ

Answer 15: Ⓒ

Concept: • Algebraic operations

Substitute two numbers such that $n > 1$. In the solutions below, the values 3 and 4 are used.

   I. $n^2 - 3n$

      Substitute 3: $3^2 - 3(3) = 0$

      Substitute 4: $4^2 - 3(4) = 4$

      The expression increases. At this point, you can eliminate choices (A), (D), and (E).

  II. $n + \dfrac{1}{n}$

      Substitute 3: $3 + \dfrac{1}{3} = 3\dfrac{1}{3}$

      Substitute 4: $4 + \dfrac{1}{4} = 4\dfrac{1}{4}$

      The expression increases. You can now eliminate choice (B). The remaining correct answer is choice (C). If you need to confirm this choice, test out expression III.

 III. $\dfrac{1}{n + 1}$

      Substitute 3: $\dfrac{1}{3 + 1} = \dfrac{1}{4}$

      Substitute 4: $\dfrac{1}{4 + 1} = \dfrac{1}{5}$

      The expression decreases.

Answer 16: Ⓓ

Concept: • Rectangle geometry

Let the area of the original rectangle $= lw$. Then, the area of the enlarged rectangle would be $2l(2w)$ or $4lw$, which is an increase of $3lw$: $4lw - lw = 3lw$.

$$\frac{\text{increase}}{\text{original}} = \frac{3lw}{lw} = 3$$

    An increase of threefold is 300%.

You can also experiment with numbers. Suppose the original width is 1 and the length is 2, for an area of 2 square units. Now, double the width and length to 2 and 4 for an area of 8 square units. The ratio of the increase 6 to the original area 2 is $\dfrac{6}{2}$, which equals 3 or 300%.

17. The equations $a^2 + 4b = 16$ and $3a^2 + 12b = 48$ are plotted on two graphs. All of the following points will lie on both graphs EXCEPT

(A) $(0, 4)$
(B) $(-4, 0)$
(C) $(2, 3)$
(D) $(3, -2)$
(E) $(-6, -5)$

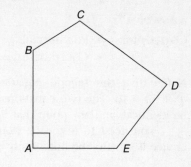

18. In pentagon *ABCDE*, if $\overline{AB} \perp \overline{AE}$, then $m\angle B + m\angle C + m\angle D + m\angle E =$

(A) $450°$
(B) $540°$
(C) $630°$
(D) $720°$
(E) $820°$

17. Ⓐ Ⓑ Ⓒ Ⓓ Ⓔ

18. Ⓐ Ⓑ Ⓒ Ⓓ Ⓔ

Answer 17: Ⓓ

Concepts: • Polynomials
           • Coordinate geometry

Notice that the second equation can be simplified (by dividing by 3) to $a^2 + 4b = 16$. The two equations are equivalent. This means their graphs must be identical, and any point that lies on one graph lies on the other.

You need to test each point in only one equation to see whether the choice is satisfied by both. Only choice (D), point $(3, -2)$, does not check out.

$$(3)^2 + 4(-2) = 16$$
$$9 - 8 \neq 16$$

You can be sure there will always be at least one PSAT question where you will have to change signs. For example, $+4(-2)$ becomes -8. Be careful of sign changes, especially in problems involving factoring.

Answer 18: Ⓐ

Concept: • Geometry

The trick in this problem is to divide the pentagon into triangles, making a bizarre shape look manageable:

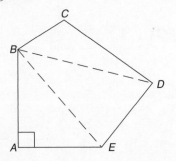

The reference information tells you that "the sum of the measures in degrees of the angles of a triangle is 180." Therefore, because there are three triangles formed, $m\angle A + m\angle B + m\angle C + m\angle D + m\angle E = 3 \times 180° = 540°$.

But don't be fooled into answering 540°, choice (B). The question asks for the sum of the measures of all angles *except* $\angle A$. Since $\overline{AB} \perp \overline{AE}$, $m\angle A = 90°$

$$m\angle B + m\angle C + m\angle D + m\angle E = 540° - 90° = 450°, \text{ choice (A).}$$

19. Racine Cameras offers a 15% discount for purchases made during its sale and an additional 3% discount if payment is made in cash. Assuming both discounts apply, how much will a $450 camera cost?

(A) $369.00
(B) $371.03
(C) $371.05
(D) $382.50
(E) $432.00

20. What is $n^3 - 9n$ divided by $n^3 + 6n^2 + 9n$?

(A) $n(n - 3)$

(B) $\dfrac{n(n - 3)}{n + 3}$

(C) $\dfrac{n - 3}{n - 3}$

(D) $\dfrac{n + 3}{n + 3}$

(E) $\dfrac{n - 3}{n + 3}$

19. Ⓐ Ⓑ Ⓒ Ⓓ Ⓔ

20. Ⓐ Ⓑ Ⓒ Ⓓ Ⓔ

Answer 19: Ⓑ

Concept: • Percentages with discounts

This is a good problem to solve with your calculator. Remember to punch in *either* the percent key [%] *or* rename the percent as decimal form (85% = .85).

A discount is a percent deducted from a marked price. Since the marked price is considered to be 100%, the first discounted price is 100% − 15% = 85%, or 85% of the marked price.

$$85\% \text{ of } \$450 = .85(450) = \$382.50$$

The intermediate price is $382.50, choice (D). The second discount is 100% (of the intermediate price) − 3% = 97%. After the second discount, then,

$$97\% \text{ of } \$382.50 = .97(382.50) = 371.025 = \$371.03$$

The final sale price is choice (B), $371.03. Choice (A) is erroneously arrived at by adding 15% and 3% together, subtracting from 100%, and multiplying— instead of figuring the first discount based on the original marked price and the second discount based on the intermediate price. Choice (E) subtracts the percentage amounts, not the dollar amounts, from the original price.

Answer 20: Ⓔ

Concepts: • Polynomials
        • Factoring

Use factoring and dividing to solve the problem. First write the problem as

$$\frac{n^3 - 9n}{n^3 + 6n^2 + 9n}$$

Note that both numerator and denominator can be factored.

$$\frac{n(n^2 - 9)}{n(n^2 + 6n + 9)} = \frac{n(n + 3)(n - 3)}{n(n + 3)(n + 3)} = \frac{(n - 3)}{(n + 3)}$$

SECTION 3: CRITICAL READING

DIRECTIONS: Each of the following sentences has one or two blanks, each blank representing a word or words needed to finish the sentence. Each sentence is followed by five words or sets of words, marked (A) through (E). From these five choices, pick the one that best completes the meaning of the sentence as a whole.

1. The students were baffled, _____, by the astronomy professor's lecture on black holes because they could not understand how light could be affected by the pull of gravity.

    (A) hypnotized
    (B) lulled
    (C) mystified
    (D) preoccupied
    (E) inspired

2. The purpose of the cooling system of an automobile is to _____ the heat generated by the engine.

    (A) coagulate
    (B) dissipate
    (C) embellish
    (D) dilapidate
    (E) permit

---

1. (A) (B) (C) (D) (E)

2. (A) (B) (C) (D) (E)

Answer 1:   Ⓒ

This is a **definition** sentence. First, eliminate the obviously wrong choices. You are looking for a word that goes along with, or means the same as, the word *baffled*. If one is baffled, one is perplexed, which is not the same as being *hypnotized*, choice (A), *lulled*, choice (B), *preoccupied*, choice (D), or *inspired*, choice (E). Choice (C), *mystified*, is very close to a synonym for the word *baffled* and therefore is the correct answer.

Answer 2:   Ⓑ

This is a **cause-and-effect** sentence. A *cooling system* would logically cause *heat* to lessen in some way, which would happen if it *dissipated*. Also, you need not know anything about automobile engines to know that it sounds strange to speak of heat *coagulating, embellishing,* or *dilapidating*, and it would not make sense to say that anything *permit*[ted] *the heat generated by the engine*. Therefore, the only logical answer is choice (B).

3. There were squirrels in the attic, scurrying about above our heads all night, _____ our sleep so that the next morning we felt exhausted.

   (A) desecrating
   (B) denying
   (C) delegating
   (D) disturbing
   (E) enhancing

4. In his backyard, Harold Wimms built a slender tower from glittering _____ of broken glass, which many neighbors considered an eyesore but which I, by contrast, considered _____.

   (A) lumps . . . detestable
   (B) remnants . . . pathetic
   (C) threads . . . meaningful
   (D) slivers . . . myopic
   (E) shards . . . exquisite

3. Ⓐ Ⓑ Ⓒ Ⓓ Ⓔ

4. Ⓐ Ⓑ Ⓒ Ⓓ Ⓔ

Answer 3:   D

This sentence deals with **cause and effect**. Here, eliminating the obviously wrong answers is the only step you need to take. Sleep isn't sacred, so it can't be *desecrated*, choice (A). The *scampering* of squirrels can't logically *deny* or *delegate* anything, choices (B) and (C), and if sleep were *enhanced*, choice (E), the people would not wake up *exhausted*. Sleep can be *disturbed* by the scampering of squirrels, so the logical answer is choice (D).

Answer 4:   E

You are given lots of help by the writer of this sentence, especially with the phrase *which I, by contrast*. You know immediately that, for the second blank, you are looking for a word that **contrasts** with *eyesore*; it will probably be a very positive word. You can almost certainly rule out choices (A), (B), and (D), all of which are negative words. Now look at the first word in the sets of choices that are left: choices (C) and (E). *Threads* of glass? No. *Shards* of glass? Yes.

5. A recent study shows that the _____ pride that map-makers sometimes take in their own countries causes them to _____ those countries as larger than they really are.

- **(A)** inflated . . . depict
- **(B)** impressive . . . wield
- **(C)** inverted . . . denounce
- **(D)** unbridled . . . dispense
- **(E)** compounded . . . detect

6. Veterinarians believe that dogs constantly kept in kennels develop behavior problems stemming from boredom, due to the _____ of their everyday lives.

- **(A)** servility
- **(B)** monotony
- **(C)** precocity
- **(D)** ferocity
- **(E)** regret

5. Ⓐ Ⓑ Ⓒ Ⓓ Ⓔ

6. Ⓐ Ⓑ Ⓒ Ⓓ Ⓔ

Answer 5:   (A)

This is a **cause-and-effect** sentence: Quickly read for the overall meaning, then try inserting each of the five sets of words into the two blanks. Immediately, choice (A) makes sense and seems reasonable, and the words are logical in context (to have *inflated* pride makes perfect sense, and map-makers do *depict* countries). Regarding choice (B), one could, I suppose, have *impressive* pride, but one could not *wield* a country. To have *inverted* pride makes little sense, choice (C). One could have *unbridled* pride, choice (D), but one could not be said to *dispense* a country. To have *compounded* pride, choice (E), makes little sense, and to *detect* a country does not seem logical.

Answer 6:   (B)

This is a **cause-and-effect** sentence. You must look among the choices for a condition that would cause *boredom*. You can immediately rule out choices (C) and (D). Choice (A) is tempting because some people regard dogs as *servile*, but even if that were true (which it isn't), *boredom* wouldn't be the result. Regarding choice (E), a dog kept in a kennel may *regret* its condition—though that is a stretch. The logical answer, then, is *monotony*.

7. Some people believe that the proliferation of computers in the twentieth century will have effects that are significant and far-reaching, as _____ as the invention of the printing press.

   (A) ingratiating
   (B) simplistic
   (C) proprietary
   (D) relegated
   (E) momentous

7. Ⓐ Ⓑ Ⓒ Ⓓ Ⓔ

Answer 7: (E)

This is a **definition** sentence. To answer the question, you need to look for a word that is synonymous with *significant and far-reaching*, so all choices can be ruled out except the last, *momentous*.

DIRECTIONS: The passages below are followed by questions based on their content. Answer the questions on the basis of what is *stated* or *implied* in each passage.

Questions 8–16 are based on the following passage.

American Canvas—Americans and the Arts
(U.S. Government National Endowment for the Arts document)

Line   "I think our greatest failure," Barbara Nicholson declared at the American
Canvas forum in Columbus, Ohio, "has been that we have allowed the arts
to be put into a little black box. The reality is that there is not a person,
whether they recognize it or not, that did not make some artistic decisions
5   from the time they opened their eyes as they moved through the day."
        Nicholson, director of the Martin Luther King, Jr., Performing and
Cultural Arts Complex in Columbus, raised a theme that resonated throughout the six American Canvas forums. In enshrining art within the temples
of culture—the museum, the concert hall, the proscenium stage—we may
10   have lost touch with the spirit of art, its direct relevance to our lives. In
building an intricate network of public and private support for thousands
of institutions over the past four decades, we may have stressed the spe-
cialized, professional aspects of the arts at the expense of their more per-
vasive, participatory nature. In the process, art became something that we
15   watch other people, usually highly skilled professionals, do rather than
something we do ourselves. "We may have nipped off the very grass roots
of support that we need now," conceded Henry Moran, executive director
of the Mid-America Arts Alliance at the San Antonio forum, "and that may
have come about from our fascination with the role of institutions within
20   the cultural ecology."
        Institutions, after all, raise the money, sell the tickets, send out the
press packets, present the art, and generally squeak the loudest when the
wheels of culture need lubrication. And they're the source of civic
pride—the buildings that adorn the covers of chamber of commerce
25   pamphlets and the festivals that are touted in tourist brochures. They're
where we take the in-laws when they come to town for a visit. We're
proud of these arts institutions, and for good reason. But these same
institutions may be obscuring our vision of the essence of art, too, the
one-to-one relationship with the creative process that all Americans,
30   whether they realize it or not, have every day of their lives. "I've never
been in a home that didn't have art in it," observed Steven Lavine,
president of the California Institute of the Arts, at the Los Angeles forum,
"[but] a lot of people . . . have the experience of having been told by the
appearance of what we used to call the 'elite organizations' that what they
35   are engaged in isn't the arts."

This process begins when we are very young, according to William
Wilson, a folklorist at Brigham Young University and a participant in the
Salt Lake City forum. Recalling his own personal background—coming
from a family of railroaders, with childhood memories full of storytelling,
40   singing, and holiday feasts—Wilson noted that for all of their creative
aspects, these activities never earned the mantle of art. "Through all of the
years of my public education," Wilson recounted, "no teacher ever
suggested to me that what I had experienced in my family . . . was of any
artistic worth. Art was something we read about in books, not a crucial
45   part of our own lives."

A half-continent away and rooted in traditions even further afield,
Gerald Yoshitomi faced very much the same homogenizing influence as a
youngster. "I remember as a child growing up," Yoshitomi, the director of
the Japanese American Cultural and Community Center, recalled at the Los
50   Angeles forum, ". . . there [were] a lot of Japanese-American arts around
me day to day, and in my home was Japanese art . . . But as I went to
school and I was educated, I was told that wasn't art. Art was something
done by someone else. By another culture basically . . ."

That failure to help our children make the connection between the
55   expressive activities in the home and the admittedly more formal,
professional cultural traditions that may (or may not) have been included
in the curriculum is one that costs us dearly. The childhood experiences of
Wilson and Yoshitomi, by no means rare, are symptomatic of the
"black-box" compartmentalization of American culture. In treating art as
60   essentially special and separate, we've failed to develop a vital link
between the classroom and the home, one that could only enhance the
educational process. So, too, have we failed to make a connection
between participation and appreciation, between active involvement in
our culture and the more passive spectatorship, prevalent in children's
65   media especially, that threatens to undermine that culture.

8. The primary focus of the passage is on

(A) the damage done to our children, and to art itself, by our enshrining of art within our cultural institutions, thus cutting ourselves off from active participation.

(B) our children's failure to become involved in the arts in school and at home and their willingness to passively view it rather than actively participate in it.

(C) the failure of our cultural institutions to allow us and our children to actively participate in art in our homes.

(D) our failure to properly fund the arts so that we can continue to enjoy them, both in our cultural institutions and in our own homes.

(E) our basic devaluing of the arts so that they are no longer a vital part of our cultural or our educational institutions.

9. Which of the following places comes closest to that which the author means by the "black box" (lines 3 and 59)?

(A) A prison
(B) A museum
(C) A school
(D) A church
(E) A private home

8. Ⓐ Ⓑ Ⓒ Ⓓ Ⓔ

9. Ⓐ Ⓑ Ⓒ Ⓓ Ⓔ

Answer 8:   (A)

Look at the key words, *enshrining* and *participation*. Choices (B) and (C) are incorrect because nowhere does the passage mention that our children or our cultural institutions have "failed." Choice (D) is incorrect because, although lack of funding is hinted at, it is not emphasized. Choice (E) is incorrect because the essay does not speak of devaluing the arts.

Answer 9:   (B)

The essay makes much of our enshrining the arts in such places as museums, cutting us off from active participation. Choices (A) and (D) are not mentioned. In the essay, choices (C) and (E) are outside the "black box."

10. In paragraph 4 of the passage, William Wilson implies that he believes that

(A) art belongs in the home, not in our public education institutions.

(B) the singing and music-playing that people do in their private homes is not really art.

(C) ordinary folks do folk art, not real art, when they tell stories and play music in their homes.

(D) art should belong to ordinary people as well as to the elite.

(E) art is not something that ordinary people readily understand, although we should give them a chance.

11. What does the final paragraph imply by the statement that today we treat the arts as something "essentially special and separate"?

(A) That art is better appreciated by specialists than by ordinary people

(B) That art belongs in a separate, special place, such as a museum or theater, rather than in a person's home

(C) That as a society we have cut ourselves off from the spirit of art

(D) That our cultural institutions desperately need help in funding the arts

(E) That we should have more reverence for the spiritual nature of art in our society

10. Ⓐ Ⓑ Ⓒ Ⓓ Ⓔ

11. Ⓐ Ⓑ Ⓒ Ⓓ Ⓔ

Answer 10: (D)

To approach this problem, remember that the question asks what Wilson *implies*, not what he directly says. Now consider the tone of paragraph 4, which indicates that he thinks his teachers were wrong when they taught that what his family did at home "wasn't art." Remember not to be too literal when answering a question about what someone probably *believes* about a certain statement. Choice (A) is incorrect because, although Wilson believes art belongs in the home, he does not necessarily believe it doesn't belong in our public institutions. Choices (B), (C), and (E) are contradicted by Williams' implications in the passage.

Answer 11: (C)

Remember to pay attention only to the final paragraph of the passage, since this is what the question refers to. Choices (A) and (B) are contradicted by the final paragraph, and choices (D) and (E) are not mentioned.

12. When Henry Moran speaks of "grass roots of support" (lines 16–17), he is referring to the support of

 (A) our country's leaders.
 (B) people in the lower classes.
 (C) ordinary people whose reverence for art remains alive today.
 (D) our elite institutions.
 (E) people who have been cut off from the arts in everyday life.

13. In line 23, the word "lubrication" most likely would include

 (A) artists who are ordinary people.
 (B) funds to support the arts.
 (C) arts education.
 (D) artistic integrity.
 (E) love of the arts.

12. Ⓐ Ⓑ Ⓒ Ⓓ Ⓔ

13. Ⓐ Ⓑ Ⓒ Ⓓ Ⓔ

Answer 12: Ⓔ

Remember the main point of the essay, which has to do with people being isolated from the arts—these people are the "grass roots." Choices (A), (B), and (C) are incorrect because the essay does not mention *our country's leaders* or *the lower classes*, nor does it imply that ordinary people have *reverence* for the arts. (D) is incorrect because the essay implies that the elite institutions do support the arts.

Answer 13: Ⓑ

Again, approach this problem by remembering that this is an *implication*, not a direct statement in the essay. The other choices would make no sense in the context of the essay.

14. Which of the following, if true, would best support the author's main argument?

   (A) Television is the wave of the future in the arts and threatens to bring art down to the level of uneducated people.

   (B) The arts are flourishing through donations from both the upper classes and ordinary citizens.

   (C) It is important to teach our children about art, but it is more important for them to learn practical survival skills.

   (D) The National Endowment for the Arts is threatened today because of what some politicians call "elitism" in the arts.

   (E) The president and the first lady of the United States enjoy visiting museums.

15. Which of the following best sums up the author's attitude toward "arts institutions" (line 27)?

   (A) Cynicism
   (B) Disgust
   (C) Unqualified admiration
   (D) Indifference
   (E) Qualified approval

---

14. Ⓐ Ⓑ Ⓒ Ⓓ Ⓔ

15. Ⓐ Ⓑ Ⓒ Ⓓ Ⓔ

Answer 14: (D)

Except for the specific mention of the NEA, this is what the essay is about. The other choices would only be peripheral to the author's argument.

Answer 15: (E)

The author says that we are proud of these institutions, *and with good reason*. But, he goes on to imply, they have robbed us of something, too. The other choices are contradicted in the essay.

16. To which of the following audiences is the essay meant to appeal most?

(A) Political leaders
(B) Educators
(C) Fund-raisers
(D) Religious leaders
(E) The news media

16. (A) (B) (C) (D) (E)

Answer 16: Ⓑ

Begin by thinking of the main point of the essay, then rule out the obviously wrong answers. Throughout, the essay speaks of the need to re-educate ourselves about the spirit of art, which is one of participation. None of the choices, besides choice (B), is emphasized at all in the essay.

Questions 17–20 are based on the following passage.

From the U.S. Government Environmental Protection Agency
Internet Home Page, November 1997

Line   Indoor pollution sources that release gases or particles into the air are the
        primary cause of indoor air quality problems in homes. Inadequate
        ventilation can increase indoor pollutant levels by not bringing in enough
        outdoor air to dilute emissions from indoor sources and by not carrying
5   indoor air pollutants out of the home. High temperature and humidity
        levels can also increase concentrations of some pollutants.
            There are many sources of indoor air pollution in any home. These
        include combustion sources such as oil, gas, kerosene, coal, wood, and
        tobacco products; building materials and furnishings as diverse as
10   deteriorated, asbestos-containing insulation; wet or damp carpet; and
        cabinetry or furniture made of certain pressed wood products; products
        for household cleaning and maintenance, personal care, or hobbies;
        central heating and cooling systems and humidification devices; and
        outdoor sources such as radon, pesticides, and outdoor air pollution.
15   The relative importance of any single source depends on how much
        of a given pollutant it emits and how hazardous those emissions are. In
        some cases, factors such as how old the source is and whether it is
        properly maintained are significant. For example, an improperly adjusted
        gas stove can emit significantly more carbon monoxide than one that is
20   properly adjusted. . . .
            The likelihood of immediate reactions to indoor air pollutants
        depends on several factors. Age and preexisting medical conditions are
        two important influences. In other cases, whether a person reacts to a
        pollutant depends on individual sensitivity, which varies tremendously
25   from person to person. Some people can become sensitized to biological
        pollutants after repeated exposures, and it appears that some people can
        become sensitized to chemical pollutants as well.
            Certain immediate effects are similar to those from colds or other
        viral diseases, so it is often difficult to determine if the symptoms are a
30   result of exposure to indoor air pollution. For this reason, it is important to
        pay attention to the time and place symptoms occur. If the symptoms fade
        or go away when a person is away from home, for example, an effort
        should be made to identify indoor air sources that may be possible causes.
        Some effects may be made worse by an inadequate supply of outdoor air
35   or from the heating, cooling, or humidity conditions prevalent in the
        home.

Other health effects may show up either years after exposure has occurred or only after long or repeated periods of exposure. These effects, which include some respiratory diseases, heart disease, and cancer, can be severely debilitating or fatal. It is prudent to try to improve the indoor air quality in your home even if symptoms are not noticeable.

17. The essay as a whole can best be summed up as

(A) a description of health hazards, meant as a warning.

(B) a diatribe against industries that pollute our atmosphere.

(C) an advertisement for pollution-prevention products.

(D) a reassuring tract that underplays pollution.

(E) a dry listing of facts about pollution.

18. Based on the essay as a whole, which of the following is the author urging us to do?

(A) Depend less on technology

(B) Visit our doctors regularly

(C) Move away from urban environments

(D) Write our congressional representatives about pollution hazards

(E) Inspect our homes for possible sources of pollution

---

17. Ⓐ Ⓑ Ⓒ Ⓓ Ⓔ

18. Ⓐ Ⓑ Ⓒ Ⓓ Ⓔ

Answer 17: (A)

Begin by glancing over the essay and noting not only its content but also the way it is organized. The essay begins with a description of sources of pollution and ends by telling us how pollution affects our health. It is not emotional in tone, as a *diatribe* would be, choice (B). It does not mention pollution-prevention products, choice (C). The mention of serious diseases caused by pollution keeps it from being either *reassuring,* choice (D), or *dry,* choice (E).

Answer 18: (E)

The author would probably agree with the other choices, but the detailed description of pollution-causing agents and devices, coupled with the last sentence of the passage, points to choice (E) as the *best* answer.

19. The main point of paragraph 5 is to remind us that

    (A) we are all in danger from pollution, no matter where we live.

    (B) our homes are more hazardous than anywhere we might visit.

    (C) it is possible for the effects of pollution to go unrecognized.

    (D) it is our own fault if we become ill from pollution

    (E) most pollutants are found indoors.

20. Which of the following best describes the organization of the essay?

    (A) A process is described, then the reason it has occurred is given.

    (B) A warning is issued, the reasons for the warning are described, then a solution is suggested.

    (C) A general principle is stated, then the reasoning behind this principle is given.

    (D) A problem is analyzed, but no solution is spelled out.

    (E) A listing of facts is made, but no attitude is taken toward the listing.

19. Ⓐ Ⓑ Ⓒ Ⓓ Ⓔ

20. Ⓐ Ⓑ Ⓒ Ⓓ Ⓔ

Answer 19: C

Remember to concentrate only on the question that is asked. Approach this question by considering only what is in paragraph 5. Ignore any mention of other choices in the essay—none of these appear in paragraph 5.

Answer 20: B

The author first warns us that indoor hazards exist, then describes the hazards in some detail, then advises us to inspect our homes regularly for those hazards. Approach this question methodically. Go down the list, reading the first phrase in each answer choice and scratching those that do not fit (for example, no *process* is described at the beginning of the essay), then moving on to the next phrase in each answer choice, and so on. Make sure all phrases are accounted for in your answer choice.

Questions 21–23 are based on the following passage.

This passage was taken from an entry in the online encyclopedia Wikipedia.

Line   *Groupthink* is a term coined by psychologist Irving Janis in 1972 to
describe one process by which a group can make bad or irrational
decisions. In a groupthink situation, each member of the group attempts
to conform his or her opinions to what they believe to be the consensus of
5   the group. This results in a situation in which the group ultimately agrees
on an action which each member might normally consider to be unwise.
One solution to the pitfall of groupthink is to appoint one group member
to play Devil's Advocate—that is, to counter each of the group decisions
with its opposite, without fear of reprisal.

21. In group decision-making, the role of the Devil's Advocate is mainly to

(A) revile the group's decision.

(B) contradict the group's decision.

(C) agree with the group's decision.

(D) nullify the group's decision.

(E) speed up the group's decision.

22. What is the meaning of "consensus" as used in the passage (line 4)?

(A) Manipulation

(B) Theory

(C) Commandment

(D) Censure

(E) Concurrence

21. Ⓐ Ⓑ Ⓒ Ⓓ Ⓔ

22. Ⓐ Ⓑ Ⓒ Ⓓ Ⓔ

Answer 21: (B)

The passage states that the Devil's Advocate's role is to *counter* (that is, to argue against) the group's decision. Choice (A) is wrong because one can argue against something without necessarily reviling it. Choices (C), (D), and (E) are wrong because the passage does not suggest that the Devil's Advocate is there to agree with, nullify, or speed up the group's decision.

Answer 22: (E)

The passage makes it clear that *Groupthink* causes conformity. The other choices are not mentioned in the passage.

23. Based on the passage, which of the following is the best example of groupthink?

   (A) A club unanimously elects a treasurer who seems honest and is someone they all like, but who shocks them later by embezzling money.

   (B) To avoid hurt feelings, a family goes on vacation together, even though each member secretly wants to stay home; the trip is a disaster.

   (C) Soldiers in a squadron dutifully obey their commander's order to take part in a dangerous mission, even though each is secretly terrified.

   (D) A corporate officer intimidates employees into working overtime without extra pay, by threatening to outsource their jobs.

   (E) A business group considers a new investment. Each member secretly examines the deal, finds it sound, and in the end the group invests.

23. Ⓐ Ⓑ Ⓒ Ⓓ Ⓔ

Answer 23: (B)

Choice (B) is the only one that satisfies the criteria for groupthink discussed in the passage: Each group member conforms, though secretly disagreeing, and a bad decision results. Choices (A) and (E) are wrong because no one secretly disagrees at the time the decisions are made. Choices (C) and (D) are wrong because the members do not conform out of desire for consensus, but out of duty in the first case, and out of fear in the second.

SECTION 4: MATHEMATICS

DIRECTIONS: This section is made up of two types of questions, multiple choice—10 questions, and Student-Produced Response—8 questions. You have 25 minutes to complete the section. You may use available space on the page for scratchwork.

NOTES:

1. You may use a calculator. All of the numbers used are real numbers.

2. You may use the figures that accompany the problems to help you find the solution. Unless the instructions say that a figure is not drawn to scale, assume that it has been drawn accurately. Each figure lies in a plane unless the instructions say otherwise.

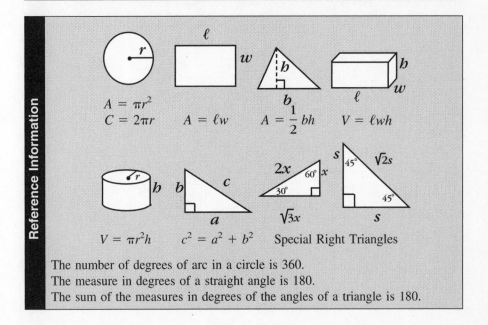

Reference Information

$A = \pi r^2$
$C = 2\pi r$

$A = \ell w$

$A = \dfrac{1}{2} bh$

$V = \ell wh$

$V = \pi r^2 h$

$c^2 = a^2 + b^2$

Special Right Triangles

The number of degrees of arc in a circle is 360.
The measure in degrees of a straight angle is 180.
The sum of the measures in degrees of the angles of a triangle is 180.

1. Simplify $4^{-\frac{3}{2}} + 64^{-\frac{1}{3}}$

   (A) $\dfrac{1}{16}$

   (B) $\dfrac{1}{8}$

   (C) $\dfrac{1}{4}$

   (D) $\dfrac{3}{8}$

   (E) $\dfrac{1}{2}$

2. Given $4x + 3y = 12 + 3y$, find x.

   (A) $3 + \dfrac{3}{2}y$

   (B) $\dfrac{1}{4}$

   (C) $\dfrac{3}{1}$

   (D) $\dfrac{1}{3}$

   (E) $12 + \dfrac{6}{2}y$

1. Ⓐ Ⓑ Ⓒ Ⓓ Ⓔ

2. Ⓐ Ⓑ Ⓒ Ⓓ Ⓔ

Answer 1:　　Ⓓ

Concepts:　　• Exponents
　　　　　　　　　• Fractions

Tackle this problem by simplifying it one step at a time. First, eliminate the negative exponents, then convert the rational exponents to their equivalent radical forms. Finally, simplify the expression to find the answer.

$$4^{-\frac{3}{2}} + 64^{-\frac{1}{3}} = \frac{1}{4^{\frac{3}{2}}} + \frac{1}{64^{\frac{1}{3}}}$$

$$= \frac{1}{(\sqrt{4})^3} + \frac{1}{\sqrt[3]{64}}$$

$$= \frac{1}{2^3} + \frac{1}{4}$$

$$= \frac{1}{8} + \frac{1}{4}$$

$$= \frac{3}{8}$$

Answer 2:　　Ⓒ

Concept:　　• Algebraic operations

Figure this one out by solving for x.

$$4x + 3y = 12 + 3y$$
$$4x = 12 + 3y - 3y$$
$$4x = 12$$
$$x = 3$$

Since 3 can also be expressed as $\frac{3}{1}$, choice (C) is the correct answer.

3. Suppose a dart is thrown at the target below in such a way that it is as likely to hit one point as another. What is the probability that the dart will land in the inner square?

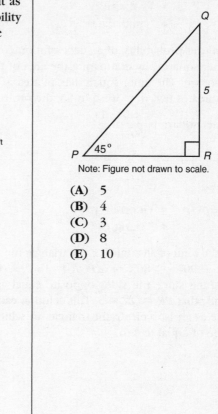

Note: Figure not drawn to scale.

(A) $\dfrac{1}{18}$

(B) $\dfrac{1}{9}$

(C) $\dfrac{1}{3}$

(D) $\dfrac{1}{2}$

(E) $\dfrac{1}{1}$

4. Given the following diagram, find the length of $\overline{PR}$.

Note: Figure not drawn to scale.

(A) 5
(B) 4
(C) 3
(D) 8
(E) 10

3. Ⓐ Ⓑ Ⓒ Ⓓ Ⓔ

4. Ⓐ Ⓑ Ⓒ Ⓓ Ⓔ

Answer 3: Ⓑ

Concepts:
- Geometry
- Probability
- Quadrilaterals

We find the probability of a successful outcome—that the dart will land inside the inner square—by comparing the area of the inner square to the area of the outer square. The inner square has an area of $2 \times 2 = 4$ sq ft. The outer square has an area of $6 \times 6 = 36$ sq ft. So, the probability that the dart will land inside the inner square is $\dfrac{4}{36}$, or $\dfrac{1}{9}$.

Answer 4: Ⓐ

Concepts:
- Geometry
- Triangles

Since the total of all angles of the triangle must equal 180°, we know that $\angle PQR$ + 45° + 90° = 180°, or $\angle PQR = 180° - 135° = 45°$. This means $\angle PQR = \angle QPR$, and since the sides opposite equal angles have equal lengths, we can conclude that $PR = QR = 5$. This solution can also be derived by identifying the triangle as an isosceles right triangle, in which case the length of the two legs must be of equal length.

5. For $x = 6$, find $(x^2)^{\frac{1}{2}}$.
   - **(A)** 6
   - **(B)** 3.460
   - **(C)** 2.048
   - **(D)** 1.570
   - **(E)** 48

6. Given $2y + 4x = 24$, find x when $y = 2$.
   - **(A)** 12
   - **(B)** 7
   - **(C)** 6
   - **(D)** 5
   - **(E)** 4

5. (A) (B) (C) (D) (E)

6. (A) (B) (C) (D) (E)

Answer 5:   Ⓐ

Concept: • Exponents

You can solve this by multiplying the exponents together:

$$(x^2)^{\frac{1}{2}} = x^{\left(\frac{2}{1}\right)\left(\frac{1}{2}\right)} = x^{\frac{2}{2}} = x^1 = 6$$

Or, by converting the expression into its equivalent radical expression, you have: $\sqrt{x^2}$. Now it is easy to see that the answer is just $x = 6$.

Answer 6:   Ⓓ

Concept: • Algebraic operations

Substituting 2 for y, the expression becomes: $4 + 4x = 24$ or $4x = 20$, which simplifies to $x = 5$.

7. Given the following diagram, find α.

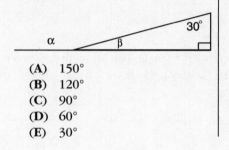

(A) 150°
(B) 120°
(C) 90°
(D) 60°
(E) 30°

8. Find the reciprocal of 0.04.

(A) 25.00
(B) 2.50
(C) 16.00
(D) 0.25
(E) 250.00

7. (A) (B) (C) (D) (E)

8. (A) (B) (C) (D) (E)

Answer 7: Ⓑ

Concepts: • Geometry
• Angle measures
• Triangles

If you recognize the triangle as a 30°-60°-90° triangle, you know that β = 60°. Now, α and β are supplementary angles, so α + β = 180°, or α = 180° − 60° = 120°.

Answer 8: Ⓐ

Concepts: • Decimals
• Fractions

Solve this problem by renaming fractions as decimals.

This problem is a snap if you use your calculator. Or, you can work it out as follows:

$$\frac{1}{.04} = \frac{1}{\left(\dfrac{4}{100}\right)}$$

$$= 1 \times \left(\frac{100}{4}\right)$$

$$= 25$$

9. A car-rental agency will rent you a car for $220 per week plus 40 cents per mile. You have budgeted $400 to spend on car rental. How many miles can you drive without exceeding your budget?

   (A) 72
   (B) 88
   (C) 100
   (D) 450
   (E) 550

10. If it takes one hour to hike one-third of a three-mile trail, how long does it take to hike one mile?

    (A) 20 minutes
    (B) 60 minutes
    (C) 40 minutes
    (D) 200 minutes
    (E) 180 minutes

9. Ⓐ Ⓑ Ⓒ Ⓓ Ⓔ

10. Ⓐ Ⓑ Ⓒ Ⓓ Ⓔ

Answer 9:   Ⓓ
Concepts: • Rates
            • Word problems
            • Algebraic operations

Solve this problem by creating a formula, a mathematical model, that uses a variable to represent the unknown quantity. Since we are asked to find the number of miles we can drive, let's make x = number of miles. We know that the total number of dollars we have budgeted for this trip is $400. We also know that the components of this total are $220 for the weekly rental plus 40 cents for every mile we drive. Our next step is to translate these words into a mathematical model, or equation, then solve for x.

$$220 + 0.40x = 400$$
$$0.40x = 400 - 220$$
$$0.40x = 180$$
$$x = \frac{180}{0.40}$$
$$x = 450$$

Answer 10:   Ⓑ
Concepts: • Rates
            • Unit conversion

Since one-third of a three-mile trail is 1 mile, which takes one hour, it takes 1 hour, or 60 minutes, to walk 1 mile.

DIRECTIONS: The following questions are student-produced responses, which require you to solve a problem and enter your answer by marking the ovals on the special grid.

(You may want to review pages 69–71 of the Student-Produced Responses unit for more detailed instructions for completing the answer grids.)

11. What whole number does

$$\frac{\dfrac{1}{5} + \dfrac{2}{3}}{\dfrac{1}{15} + \dfrac{1}{5} + \dfrac{1}{6}} \text{ equal?}$$

12. At the cookie factory, 0.4% of a batch of cookies is broken. If this batch has 8 broken cookies, how many cookies are in the batch?

11.

12.

Answer 11: 2

Concept: • Fractions

You will need to find the least common denominator in order to simplify this fraction. By quick experimentation (5×3, then 5×6), you learn that 30 is the least number that will clear all the fractions.

Multiply all terms in the fraction's numerator and denominator by 30:

$$\frac{\dfrac{1}{5} + \dfrac{2}{3}}{\dfrac{1}{15} + \dfrac{1}{5} + \dfrac{1}{6}} \times \frac{30}{30} =$$

$$\frac{6 + 20}{2 + 6 + 5} = \frac{26}{13} = 2$$

Answer 12: 2,000

Concept: • Percentages

This question can be tricky, so you need to think about what element in this percent problem is unknown. You are trying to discover the number of cookies, including the broken ones, in the entire batch.

Let x = number of cookies in the entire batch.

Then $0.4\%x$ = number of broken cookies in the batch, which you are told is 8.

$$0.4\%x = 8$$
$$.004x = 8$$

Use your calculator at this point.

$$x = \frac{8}{.004} = 2,000$$

Or, if figured by hand, you can divide the numerator and denominator by 4:

$$x = \frac{8}{.004} = \frac{2}{.001}$$

and then multiply them by 1,000:

$$x = \frac{2(1,000)}{.001(1,000)} = \frac{2,000}{1} = 2,000.$$

Be careful when renaming a percent with a decimal point. Remember to move the decimal point two places to the left to rename a percent as a decimal.

13. Four identical cylindrical candles fit exactly into a cubical box. The area of the circular top of each candle is 9π. What is the total area of all six sides of the box?

14. A reading club has 5 members. Berta is 50 years old, Tim is 46, Ned is 55, and Lila and Lola are both 42. Find the median, mode, and mean of their ages. Mark the greatest of these measures on your answer sheet.

13.

14.

Answer 13: 864

Concepts: • Trapezoids or quadralaterials
• Circle and square geometry

You are told that the area of the top of each candle (a circle) is 9π. Use the formula for the area of a circle and substitute:

$$\pi r^2 = 9\pi \qquad \text{Divide by } \pi.$$
$$r^2 = 9$$
$$r = 3 \qquad \text{Sketch a picture at this point.}$$

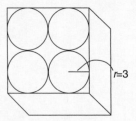

If the radius of the top of each candle is 3, the width of the crate is $4r$, or 12. You know the crate is a cube, so the area of each side is 12×12, or 144. The sum of the areas of all 6 sides is 864.

Answer 14: 47

Concept: • Median, mode, and mean (average)

If you know how to define and determine median, mode, and mean, you are practically home free on this problem. First you need to put the list of the reading club's ages in order: 42, 42, 46, 50, 55. Then figure the median, mode, and mean.

The median is the number that falls exactly in the middle of the list. As there are two numbers above 46 and two below it, the median is 46.

The mode is the number that occurs the most often. Each number occurs once, except 42, which occurs twice. Therefore, the mode of this list is 42.

Mean is another term for average. The sum of all the ages divided by the number of ages is

$$\frac{42 + 42 + 46 + 50 + 55}{5} = \frac{235}{5} = 47$$

The greatest of the these three measures is 47.

15. Mary and Larry start at the same time from cities that are 329 miles apart and drive toward each other. Mary drives steadily at 40 miles per hour, and Larry drives consistently at 54 miles per hour. In how many hours will they meet?

16. Let Set *A* consist of all multiples of 3 between 10 and 29. Let Set *B* consist of all multiples of 4 between 10 and 29. What is one possible number that is in Set *A* but *not* in Set *B*?

15.

16.

Answer 15: 3.5

Concepts: • Word problems
• Motion formula

This is a motion problem. Motion problems are based on the relationship that Rate × Time = Distance. Rate is usually given in miles per hour. Time is often given in hours, and distance is often represented by miles.

In this example, you need to find h, the number of hours it will take Mary and Larry to meet. Using the formula, $40h$ = the distance traveled by Mary and $54h$ = the distance traveled by Larry. The total distance traveled is 329 miles. Therefore,

$$40h + 54h = 329$$
$$94h = 329$$
$$h = \frac{329}{94}$$

Use your calculator here.

$$h = 3.5$$

Be sure to enter the decimal point in its own column on the grid.

Answer 16: 15 or 18 or 21 or 27

Concepts: • Sequences
• Factoring

Some questions on the PSAT may have more than one correct response. In such cases, grid-in only one answer.

You are told that Set A consists of all multiples of 3 between 10 and 29. Since the sequence is short, you can write out the entire set:

$$\{12, 15, 18, 21, 24, 27\}$$

Set B consists of all multiples of 4 between 10 and 29. You are to find a possible number that is in Set A but *not* in Set B. You might compute Set B the way you did the first set and compare the two sets. However, instead of listing all the elements of Set B, a shortcut is to simply eliminate the members of Set A that are divisible by 4 (12 and 24).

The remaining numbers—15, 18, 21, and 27—are all correct answers to this problem. Choose one and enter it on the grid.

17. $\overline{EH} \parallel \overline{FG}$, $EH = 42$, $GH = 10$, FG = 30, $EF = 10$. What is the area of trapezoid *EFGH*?

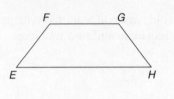

18. Let *a* and *b* be positive. If $a^2 + 2ab + b^2 = 64$, then what is the average of *a* plus *b*?

17.

18.

Answer 17: 288

Concepts: • Geometry
  • Trapezoids or quadrilaterals

When working with a figure such as a trapezoid, you will want to divide it into shapes that are easier to measure, such as a rectangle and two triangles.

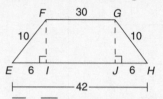

Draw $\overline{FI} \perp \overline{EH}$ and draw $\overline{GJ} \perp \overline{EH}$. The lengths of the two new triangle bases

$$EI = JH = 6 \text{ because } 42 - 30 = 12, \text{ divided by 2, equals } 6$$

ΔEFI is a 3-4-5 right triangle with $EI = 2(3)$ and $EF = 2(5)$. Therefore, FI has to equal $2(4) = 8$.

Let b = the height of the trapezoid, which is the same as FI, 8. Recall that the area of a trapezoid is $\frac{1}{2}b(FG + EH)$: $\frac{1}{2}(8)(72) = 288$. Your trapezoid's area is 288.

Answer 18: 4

Concepts: • Polynomial arithmetic
  • Square roots

You are looking for the average of a plus b, but you don't see $a + b$ in the equation. You may be thinking, "Where is $a + b$ in the expression $a^2 + 2ab + b^2 = 64$?" This line of thought may remind you of the formula of polynomial arithmetic, where the square of the sums of two numbers is written

$$(x + y)^2 = x^2 + 2xy + y^2$$

You then substitute this problem's variables, so that:

$$(a + b)^2 = a^2 + 2ab + b^2 = 64,$$

which can also be stated as

$$(a + b)^2 = 64.$$

You can now find the square root of each side.

$$a + b = \pm 8$$

Since a and b are positive by definition, $a + b = 8$. The average of a plus b, then, is

$$\frac{a + b}{2} = \frac{8}{2} = 4.$$

SECTION 5: WRITING SKILLS

DIRECTIONS: No sentence contains more than one error. The error, if there is one, is underlined and lettered; elements that are not underlined are correct. In choosing answers, follow the requirements of standard written English. If there is an error, select the one underlined part that must be changed to make the sentence correct and fill in the corresponding oval on the answer sheet. If there is no error, fill in oval E.

1. Besides fetching and dancing,
   <u>A</u>
   my dog Bob can
   <u>B</u>
   sit up, beg, shake hands, and
   <u>C</u>
   he rolls over. No error.
   <u>D</u>   <u>E</u>

2. If one prefers orange
   marmalade on one's toast, you
   <u>A</u>   <u>B</u>
   don't want to be served grape
   <u>C</u>
   jelly or kumquat jam. No error.
   <u>D</u>   <u>E</u>

1. Ⓐ Ⓑ Ⓒ Ⓓ Ⓔ

2. Ⓐ Ⓑ Ⓒ Ⓓ Ⓔ

Answer 1: Ⓓ

Type of error: Lack of parallel structure. The series *sit up, beg, shake hands*, choice (C), is parallel; however, the phrase he rolls over is not, and makes for a wordy sentence. Choice (A) is correct as part of an introductory phrase. Choice (B) is a correctly written noun with a modifier.

Answer 2: Ⓑ

Type of error: Shift in person from *one* to *you*. Choice (A) is the correct use of the preposition *on*, and choice (C) is a correctly written prepositional phrase. Choice (D) makes correct use of the conjunction *or*.

3. The language

spoken by the settlers is
$\overline{\qquad\qquad}$
   A
unrelated to any other known
  $\overline{\qquad\qquad}$
   B
tongue, so where they came
   $\overline{\quad}$
   C
from was a mystery. No error.
$\overline{\qquad\qquad}$ $\overline{\qquad\qquad}$
  D   **E**

4. Leonardo da Vinci's notebooks

were written in mirror-script,
$\overline{\qquad\qquad}$
  A
which makes them interesting
  $\overline{\qquad\qquad}$
   B
but difficult to decipher.
$\overline{\qquad}$ $\overline{\qquad\qquad}$
 C   **D**
No error.
$\overline{\qquad}$
 E

---

3. Ⓐ Ⓑ Ⓒ Ⓓ Ⓔ

4. Ⓐ Ⓑ Ⓒ Ⓓ Ⓔ

Answer 3:   Ⓓ

Type of error: Shift in tense from *is* to *was*.

Answer 4:   Ⓔ

The sentence is correctly written.

5. John Jacob Astor, one of the
world's richest and most powerful
———————————————————
             A
men, has the misfortune of being
———————   ——————————
        B
on the Titanic when it sailed on
——————
    C
its maiden voyage. No error.
——   ————
D   **E**

6. All the guests will arrive at our
              ——————————
              A
house at once, and
——————————
      B
we will dance, sing holiday
——————————————
            C
songs, and eat great quantities
—————————
      C
of food. No error.
——   ————
D   **E**

5. Ⓐ Ⓑ Ⓒ Ⓓ Ⓔ

6. Ⓐ Ⓑ Ⓒ Ⓓ Ⓔ

Answer 5: (B)

Type of error: Shift in tense from *has* (present) to *sailed* (past). Choice (A) is the correct use of comparative adjectives. Choice (C) is a correctly written prepositional phrase. Choice (D) is the correct form of *its* (the possessive, without an apostrophe).

Answer 6: (E)

The sentence is correctly written.

7. The children are very thin,
   $\overline{\hspace{1.5em}\textbf{A}\hspace{1.5em}}$
   tired, and hungry and
   $\overline{\hspace{1.5em}\textbf{A}\hspace{1.5em}}$
   haven't got no coats or boots
   $\overline{\hspace{2em}\textbf{B}\hspace{2em}}$
   to keep them warm in
   $\overline{\hspace{1em}\textbf{C}\hspace{1em}}$
   this harsh weather. No error.
   $\overline{\hspace{3em}\textbf{D}\hspace{3em}}$ $\overline{\hspace{1em}\textbf{E}\hspace{1em}}$

8. In the old days we used electric
   $\overline{\hspace{1em}\textbf{A}\hspace{1em}}$
   typewriters to perform the tasks
   $\overline{\hspace{2em}\textbf{B}\hspace{2em}}$
   now did on computers, so the
   $\overline{\hspace{1em}\textbf{C}\hspace{1em}}$
   work was more difficult.
   $\overline{\hspace{2em}\textbf{D}\hspace{2em}}$
   No error.
   $\overline{\hspace{1em}\textbf{E}\hspace{1em}}$

7. Ⓐ Ⓑ Ⓒ Ⓓ Ⓔ

8. Ⓐ Ⓑ Ⓒ Ⓓ Ⓔ

Answer 7:   (B)

Type of error: Double negative. The phrase should read *have no coats*. Choice (A) makes good use of parallel structure. Choice (C) is a correctly written prepositional phrase. Choice (D) is a correctly written noun with a modifier.

Answer 8:   (C)

Type of error: Ungrammatical use of verb. Choice (A) is a correctly written subject-verb combination. Choice (B) is a correctly written prepositional phrase. Choice (D) is the correct form of the comparative *more*.

9. The president and first lady

go jogging down Pennsylvania
_____
A
Avenue every morning,
_____
B
followed by members
_____
C
to the Secret Service. No error.
_____   _____
D   E

10. She seemed altogether
_____
A
oblivious about the storm raging
_____   _____
B   C
all around her. No error.
_____   _____
D   E

9. Ⓐ Ⓑ Ⓒ Ⓓ Ⓔ

10. Ⓐ Ⓑ Ⓒ Ⓓ Ⓔ

Answer 9:   Ⓓ

Type of error: Unidiomatic use of preposition. The correct prepositional phrase here would be *of the Secret Service*. Choice (A) is a correctly written verb form. Choice (B) is the correct adjective form. Choice (C) makes correct use of the verb and preposition.

Answer 10:   Ⓑ

Type of error: Unidiomatic usage. The correct idiom is *oblivious of*.

11. The queen has promised to give
    _____
              A
    her son's hand in marriage to
    _____
              B
    whoever slays the monster
    _____
              C
    at the gate. No error.
    _____   _____
        D   E

12. Neither Sarah or Margaret want
    _____
              A
    to go out into the woods so late
    _____ _____
         B   C
    at night. No error.
    _____ _____
       D   E

11. Ⓐ Ⓑ Ⓒ Ⓓ Ⓔ

12. Ⓐ Ⓑ Ⓒ Ⓓ Ⓔ

Answer 11: Ⓔ

There is no error in this sentence.

Answer 12: Ⓐ

Type of error: Confusion of either/or with neither/nor. Choices (B) through (D) are correctly written prepositional phrases.

13. Kristen announced that she was

    going to take a plane for Seattle
    $\overline{\text{A}}$ $\overline{\text{B}}$
    that evening and intended to
    $\overline{\text{C}}$
    stay at the Hilton. No error.
    $\overline{\text{D}}$ $\overline{\text{E}}$

14. Attempts to predict earthquakes
    $\overline{\text{A}}$
    have been made for

    centuries they continue to take
    $\overline{\text{B}}$ $\overline{\text{C}}$
    cities by surprise. No error.
    $\overline{\text{D}}$ $\overline{\text{E}}$

13. Ⓐ Ⓑ Ⓒ Ⓓ Ⓔ

14. Ⓐ Ⓑ Ⓒ Ⓓ Ⓔ

Answer 13: Ⓑ

Type of error: Unidiomatic use of preposition. The correct form is *take a plane to Seattle*. Choices (A) and (D) are correctly written prepositions. Choice (C) is the correct form of the conjunction and verb for this sentence.

Answer 14: Ⓑ

Type of error: Fused sentence. A period should go between *centuries* and *they*. Choices (A), (C), and (D) are correctly written prepositional phrases.

15. This secret is just
    A
    between you and I, because I
              B
    trust you more than I do the
         C   D
    others. No error.
                E

16. Mammoths, lions, and

    also the woolly rhinoceros were
                    A
    more frequently depicted in
                         B
    cave paintings than

    rabbits, fish, and birds, which is
                C   D
    puzzling. No error.
              E

15. Ⓐ Ⓑ Ⓒ Ⓓ Ⓔ

16. Ⓐ Ⓑ Ⓒ Ⓓ Ⓔ

Answer 15: Ⓑ

Type of error: Wrong pronoun case. The corrected phrase would read *between you and me*. Choice (A) is a correctly written modifier, *This*. Choice (C) is the correct form of the verb *trust*. Choice (D) is the correct form of the comparative *more*.

Answer 16: Ⓐ

Type of error: Lack of parallel structure. The words *also the* make for a wordy sentence and do not make use of parallel structure, which would be more effective here. Choice (B) is a correctly written verb with an adverb. Choice (C) makes use of parallel structure. Choice (D) is the correct form of the verb *is*.

17. Lie detector evidence is not
    $\overline{\text{A}}$
    admissible in court, although
    $\overline{\text{B}}$ $\overline{\text{C}}$
    it is unreliable. No error.
    $\overline{\text{D}}$ $\overline{\text{E}}$

18. Of all the girls, Marcy was the
    $\overline{\text{A}}$
    more stuck-up, so we didn't like
    $\overline{\text{B}}$ $\overline{\text{C}}$
    her at all. No error.
    $\overline{\text{D}}$ $\overline{\text{E}}$

17. Ⓐ Ⓑ Ⓒ Ⓓ Ⓔ

18. Ⓐ Ⓑ Ⓒ Ⓓ Ⓔ

Answer 17: Ⓒ

Type of error: Illogical transition. The correct transition would be *because*. Choices (A) and (D) are correct forms of the verb *is*. Choice (B) is the correct preposition for this sentence.

Answer 18: Ⓑ

Type of error: Incorrect use of comparative. Choice (A) is a correctly written introductory phrase. Choice (C) is the correct transitional word here. Choice (D) does not make the sentence wordy because it fits in with the writer's style.

19. Theres nothing I like better
     <u>A</u>
   than chocolate chip
     <u>B</u>
   cookies; I could eat them
           <u>C</u>
   morning, noon, and night.
                 <u>D</u>
   No error.
     <u>E</u>

---

19. Ⓐ Ⓑ Ⓒ Ⓓ Ⓔ

Answer 19: Ⓐ

Type of error: Missing apostrophe. *There is* should be written *There's*. *Than* is the correct form of the preposition in choice (B). The semicolon correctly divides two main clauses in choice (C). Choice (D) has parallel structure.

DIRECTIONS: Part or all of the following numbered sentences are underlined. Beneath each are five choices. The first choice is to leave the sentence as is; the other four choices show ways to rephrase the underlined portions. The portions that are not underlined should remain the same. Choose the most effective version of each sentence.

20. Substantial ruins of fifth-century churches can be found in northern Syria.

 (A) (As it is now)
 (B) Fifth-century churches can be found in northern Syria, they are in substantial ruins.
 (C) You can find substantial ruins of fifth-century churches; in northern Syria.
 (D) In northern Syria, it can be found that there are substantial ruins of fifth-century churches.
 (E) Substantial ruins of fifth-century churches, can be found in northern Syria.

21. As we walked through the forest, a voice calling us, sweet and clear.

 (A) (As it is now)
 (B) a voice calls us
 (C) a voice is calling us
 (D) a voice called us
 (E) calling us, we heard a voice

20. (A) (B) (C) (D) (E)

21. (A) (B) (C) (D) (E)

Answer 20: (A)

The sentence is correct as is.

Answer 21: (D)

Type of error: Missing subject. Choice (A) is a fragment. Choices (B) and (C) represent a change in tense from past to present. Choice (E) is unnecessarily convoluted and wordy.

22. If you leave first thing in the morning, <u>you should arrive</u> by 5 o'clock.

    (A) (As it is now)
    (B) you have arrived
    (C) you will arrived
    (D) you arrived
    (E) you should be arriving

23. <u>Why have I come all this way and for nothing?</u>

    (A) (As it is now)
    (B) Why have I come all this way for nothing?
    (C) I have come all this way for nothing, why?
    (D) For nothing, I have come all this way, and why?
    (E) Why have I come, all this way for nothing?

---

22. Ⓐ Ⓑ Ⓒ Ⓓ Ⓔ

23. Ⓐ Ⓑ Ⓒ Ⓓ Ⓔ

Answer 22: (A)

The sentence is correct as it is.

Answer 23: (B)

Type of error: Wordiness and grammatical and punctuation errors. The word *and* clutters up the sentence, choice (A). Choice (C) is a fused sentence. Choice (D) is unnecessarily convoluted. Choice (E) has an unnecessary comma.

24. Our house is set back from the road amid brambles <u>and it has poison oak</u>.

    (A) (As it is now)
    (B) and poison oak.
    (C) and there is poison oak.
    (D) and poison oak is there also.
    (E) and it has got poison oak.

25. <u>Why did John, bring his dog to the wedding?</u>

    (A) (As it is now)
    (B) Why did, John, bring his dog to the wedding?
    (C) Why did John bring his dog to the wedding?
    (D) Why did John bring, his dog, to the wedding?
    (E) Why did John bring his dog, to the wedding?

---

24. Ⓐ Ⓑ Ⓒ Ⓓ Ⓔ

25. Ⓐ Ⓑ Ⓒ Ⓓ Ⓔ

Answer 24: (B)

Type of error: Wordiness. The other choices are unnecessarily wordy.

Answer 25: (C)

Type of error: Superfluous punctuation. The other choices have unnecessary commas.

26. A black dwarf; is the final stage of a star after it has run out of energy.

   (A) (As it is now)
   (B) A black dwarf is the final stage of a star; after it has run out of energy.
   (C) A black dwarf is the final stage of a star after it has run out of energy.
   (D) A black dwarf: is the final stage of a star after it has run out, of energy.
   (E) A black dwarf is, the final stage of a star, after it has run out of energy.

27. The wind made an eerie sound, we became frightened.

   (A) (As it is now)
   (B) The wind made an eerie sound; we became frightened.
   (C) The wind, made an eerie sound, we became frightened.
   (D) The wind made, an eerie sound, we became frightened.
   (E) The wind made an eerie sound; we became: frightened.

26. Ⓐ Ⓑ Ⓒ Ⓓ Ⓔ

27. Ⓐ Ⓑ Ⓒ Ⓓ Ⓔ

Answer 26: Ⓒ

Type of error: Unnecessary punctuation and grammatical error. Choice (A) has a comma between the subject and the verb. Choice (B) has a colon between an independent and a dependent clause. Choice (D) misuses the colon, which is supposed to introduce a statement or precede a list. Choice (E) has superfluous commas.

Answer 27: Ⓑ

Type of error: Comma splice. Choice (A) is a comma splice. Choice (C) has a comma between the subject and the verb and is a comma splice. Choices (D) and (E) have superfluous punctuation.

28. <u>Prior to the time that I arrived,</u>
<u>they had done most of the</u>
<u>redecorating involving a great</u>
<u>deal of expense.</u>

- **(A)** (As it is now)
- **(B)** Prior to the time I arrived,
  they did most of the
  expensive decorating,
  involving a great deal of
  cost.
- **(C)** Before I arrived, they had
  done most of the redecorating, involving a great
  deal of expense.
- **(D)** Prior to my arrival, they
  did most of the very costly
  redecorating, involving a
  great deal of expense.
- **(E)** Before I arrived, they did
  most of the expensive
  redecorating.

29. Do you know that the cause <u>or</u>
<u>reason for dental decay in</u>
<u>people with bad teeth</u> is
heredity?

- **(A)** (As it is now)
- **(B)** reason for dental decay in
  people with bad teeth
- **(C)** of dental decay in people
  with bad teeth
- **(D)** for dental decay
- **(E)** of dental decay

28. Ⓐ Ⓑ Ⓒ Ⓓ Ⓔ

29. Ⓐ Ⓑ Ⓒ Ⓓ Ⓔ

Answer 28: (E)

Type of error: Wordiness. Choices (A) through (D) are wordy.

Answer 29: (E)

Type of error: Wordiness. Choices (A) through (C) are wordy. Choice (D) uses the wrong preposition *for*.

30. Where have you <u>gone, my dear</u> little cat?

 (A) (As it is now)
 (B) gone? My dear
 (C) gone. My dear
 (D) gone; my dear
 (E) gone my dear

31. Eleanor's lips parted <u>on a thin smile</u>.

 (A) (As it is now)
 (B) to a thin smile
 (C) for a thin smile
 (D) at a thin smile
 (E) in a thin smile

30. Ⓐ Ⓑ Ⓒ Ⓓ Ⓔ

31. Ⓐ Ⓑ Ⓒ Ⓓ Ⓔ

Answer 30: (A)

There is no punctuation error in this sentence.

Answer 31: (E)

Type of error: Unidiomatic use of prepositions. All choices except (E) make the same error.

32. Her broad, rather flat <u>face;</u>
<u>nevertheless was</u> beautiful.

(A) (As it is now)
(B) face nevertheless was
(C) face, nevertheless was
(D) face. Nevertheless was
(E) face, nevertheless, it was

33. Robert took Vernon to a
baseball <u>game; he</u> had never
seen one before.

(A) (As it is now)
(B) game; Vernon
(C) game, he
(D) game Vernon
(E) game. Who

32. Ⓐ Ⓑ Ⓒ Ⓓ **Ⓔ**

33. Ⓐ Ⓑ Ⓒ Ⓓ **Ⓔ**

Answer 32: Ⓑ

Type of error: Sentence fragment. In choice (A), a semicolon separates an independent and a dependent clause, making the sentence a fragment. Choice (C) would be correct if a comma were placed after *nevertheless* to set off the parenthetical phrase. Choices (D) and (E) represent a comma splice.

Answer 33: Ⓑ

Choices (A), (C), and (E) represent vague pronoun references; the reader cannot tell whether it is Robert or Vernon who has never seen a game. Choice (D) is a run-on sentence.

DIRECTIONS: Read the passage below and answer the questions that come after it. Some of the questions will ask you to improve sentence structure and word choice. Other questions will refer to parts of the essay or to the entire essay and ask you to improve organization and development.

(1) *An ecosystem is a community of animals and plants interacting with one another and with their physical environment.* (2) *The key word here is "community."* (3) *From urban settings to rural countryside, the landscape is alive with the beauty and detail of nature.* (4) *The ecosystems that you see support you with resources (timber, water, components of pharmaceuticals, and food, just to name a few) and services (water purification and erosion control, for example), making your survival possible and your life more enjoyable.* (5) *It is essential to the survival of the human family that we protect the fragile network that makes up the ecosystem within which we live.*

(6) *It is also important to remember that humans are only one member of an ecosystem, every ecosystem includes a multitude of other plants and animals.* (7) *This is most obvious with amphibians and migratory birds.* (8) *Frogs and salamanders develop in the water but spend much of their adult lives on land.* (9) *A wood duck may winter in the Everglades, feed and rest in a Virginia pond, and nest in an upstate New York swamp.* (10) *The survival of such species is dependent on the availability and environmental condition of all the required habitats—at the right time and place.* (11) *We should always keep in mind other species' reliance on local ecosystems.* (12) *When evaluating the benefits these ecosystems provide our human communities.*

34. Which of the following best describes the organization of the materials in the passage?

- **(A)** A definition is given, appeals to the reader's emotion and self-interest are made, then advice is given on how to approach some problem.
- **(B)** An account of a process is given, followed by a reason for its occurrence.
- **(C)** A set of examples is given, then a conclusion is drawn.
- **(D)** A statement of principals is given, then a solution is proposed.
- **(E)** A set of examples is given, then a conclusion is drawn from them.

35. Which of the following would be the next logical topic in the discussion of ecosystems in the passage?

- **(A)** A more in-depth discussion of things the reader could do to protect the environment
- **(B)** A discussion of the pharmaceuticals our ecosystem provides for us
- **(C)** A discussion of Darwin's theory of survival of the fittest
- **(D)** A discussion of how the term *ecosystem* was arrived at
- **(E)** A discussion of the beauty of nature

34. Ⓐ Ⓑ Ⓒ Ⓓ Ⓔ

35. Ⓐ Ⓑ Ⓒ Ⓓ Ⓔ

Answer 34: (A)

The definition of an ecosystem is presented first, followed by a description of how the ecosystem we live in affects us, then advice is given on keeping the ecosystem healthy. The other choices do not describe the organization of this passage.

Answer 35: (A)

The passage is an appeal to the reader to protect the ecosystem, and choice (A) is most relevant to that. Choices (B), (D), and (E) are too narrow. Choice (C) is irrelevant.

36. Which of the following sentences would make the best transition between sentences (2) and (3)?

   (A) Look out your window and consider the world around you.
   (B) The word "community" is practically meaningless nowadays.
   (C) Is it possible to save the earth at this late date?
   (D) Science has perhaps done more harm than good to our communities.
   (E) We should be practical, not sentimental, in our approach to the environment.

37. Which of the following is the best way to revise the underlined portion of sentence (6), reproduced below?

   It is also important to remember that humans are only one member of an ecosystem, every ecosystem includes a multitude of other plants and animals.

   (A) (As it is now)
   (B) ecosystem. Every
   (C) ecosystem, or every
   (D) ecosystem, although every
   (E) ecosystem every

36. Ⓐ Ⓑ Ⓒ Ⓓ Ⓔ

37. Ⓐ Ⓑ Ⓒ Ⓓ Ⓔ

Answer 36: (A)

Sentence (3) appeals to the reader to look at the beauty of the ecosystems outside. Choices (B) and (C) are more negative in tone than the rest of the essay. Choices (D) and (E) run counter to the author's general attitude. For instance, regarding choice (D), the mention of pharmaceuticals (products of science) has a positive tone. Regarding choice (E), the author seems to invite sentiment in his description of the beauty of nature.

Answer 37: (B)

Choice (A) is a comma splice. Choices (C) and (D) contain illogical transitions. Choice (E) is a fused sentence.

38. Which of the following sentences would most logically and effectively introduce the ideas expressed in sentence (8)?

  (A) Some species depend on more than one habitat.
  (B) Some species are less appealing than others.
  (C) Some species grow in accordance with the works of Darwin.
  (D) Amphibians, such as frogs and salamanders, are cold-blooded.
  (E) Some species, such as amphibians, do not migrate.

39. What is the best way to revise and combine sentences (11) and (12), reproduced below?

We should always keep in mind other species' reliance on local ecosystems. When evaluating the benefits these ecosystems provide our human communities.

  (A) (As it is now)
  (B) ecosystems when
  (C) ecosystems and when
  (D) ecosystems; when
  (E) ecosystems, but when

38. Ⓐ Ⓑ Ⓒ Ⓓ Ⓔ

39. Ⓐ Ⓑ Ⓒ Ⓓ Ⓔ

Answer 38: Ⓐ

This is the only sentence that is related to the fact that frogs and salamanders develop in water but spend most of their lives on land. The other choices are irrelevant.

Answer 39: Ⓑ

In choices (A) and (D), sentence (12) is a fragment. Choices (C) and (E) contain the illogical transitional words *and* and *but*.

THE NEW SAT

What Does It Mean for You?

You may have heard that the SAT is going to change. But when will it happen? How will it change? And most importantly, what does it all mean for you?

WHEN?

The test in question is the SAT I: Reasoning Test, commonly referred to as just the plain old SAT. The modified SAT will be introduced in March 2005. If you will be a high school senior graduating and looking to enter college in 2006, you will take the new exam. If you will be a high school senior graduating and looking to enter college before 2006, you will take the current version of the exam.

WHAT?

The current SAT consists of two sections, Verbal and Math. Changes will be made to each of the existing sections, and a new Writing section will be created. Some of the changes relate to the actual content being tested, while others relate to the question types used to test it.

VERBAL

The first change to the Verbal section is its name. On the new SAT, this section will be called Critical Reading (as in the new PSAT). This change signals the recognition of the importance of reading as a part of high school curricula and as a skill vital to success in college. This focus will be carried through to the content of the section. The second change to the Verbal section is the elimination of the analogy questions. Analogies require students to detect the relationship between a pair of words in the question stem and then to select the pair of words in the answer choices that reflects the same relationship. This question type is being eliminated so that this section on the new exam will consist entirely of critical reading questions, which will test reading skills at the sentence, paragraph, and passage level. The third change to the Verbal section is the addition of paragraph-length critical reasoning questions, to supplement the existing question types of sentence completions and reading comprehension passages. The topics of the given texts will represent a wide range of subjects, including science, literature, humanities, and history.

MATH

The Math section of the SAT will also change. Algebra II material will be tested on the new exam in order to better align the SAT with the math curriculum being taught in high school classrooms. Since most high school students in general and the vast majority of college-bound high school students complete Algebra II, it makes sense for this content to be a part of the exam. It also makes sense since most four-year colleges require three years of high school math.

The second change to the Math section is the elimination of quantitative comparisons. This question type requires students to compare quantities in two columns and decide if one or the other is greater, if they are equal, or if it is impossible to determine based on the information given. The other two current math question types, 5-choice multiple-choice and student-produced responses, will remain on the exam.

WRITING

ESSAY

The biggest change to the SAT will be the introduction of a new Writing section. This change is designed to provide an additional measure for college admissions purposes as well as to emphasize the importance of writing for success in school and professional life. The Writing section will consist of two parts: an essay and a multiple-choice section. Students will be given 25 minutes to respond to a prompt and construct a well-organized essay that effectively addresses the task. The essay question may require students to complete a statement, to react to a quote or excerpt, or to agree or disagree with a point of view. In any case, a good essay will support the chosen position with specific reasons and examples from literature, history, art, science, current affairs, or even a student's own experiences.

Essays will be scored based on the procedures for the current SAT II: Writing Test. Essays will be graded by two independent readers on a scale of 1-6, and their two scores will be combined to form an essay subscore that ranges from 2 to 12. Should the readers' scores vary by more than 2 points, a third reader will score the essay. The readers will be high school teachers and college professors who teach composition. They will score essays using a rubric that evaluates the compositions based upon how effectively the task in the question is addressed, how well the essay is organized, the use of appropriate examples, the facility of language, and the variety of sentence structure and vocabulary. To ensure that essays will be scored in a timely manner, they will be scanned and sent to readers via the Internet for grading purposes.

MULTIPLE-CHOICE

The Writing section will also include multiple-choice grammar and usage questions. Some of these questions will call upon students to improve given sentences and paragraphs. Others will present students with sentences and require them to identify mistakes in diction, grammar, sentence construction, subject-verb agreement, proper word usage, and wordiness. Questions like this already appear on both the SAT II: Writing Test and the Writing Skills section of the PSAT.

The highest possible score on the new Writing section will be 800. Scores on the essay and multiple-choice section will be combined to produce a single score. A writing subscore will also be assigned. The highest possible scores on the Critical Reading and Math sections will remain 800 each, making a perfect score on the new SAT 2400.

WHY?

These changes to the SAT come on the heels of complaints by educators about the current exam. They assert that the SAT as it stands is not an accurate enough indicator of the content taught in high school classrooms. The test has also been accused of being biased against less affluent students. The College Board has stated that it has three goals in revising the exam:

- To better align it with high school curricula and college requirements

- To provide college admissions officers with a measure of a student's writing skills

- To emphasize how crucial writing is to success in college and beyond

CHANGES AT A GLANCE

Critical Reading	Current SAT I	New SAT I
Time	Two 30-minute sections One 15-minute section Total: 75 minutes	Two 25-minute sections One 20-minute section Total: 70 minutes
Content	Analogical reasoning Critical reading Sentence-level reading	Critical reading Sentence-level reading
Question Types	Analogies Reading comprehension Sentence completions	Reading comprehension Sentence completions Paragraph-length critical reading
Score	200–800	200–800

Math	Current SAT I	New SAT I
Time	Two 30-minute sections One 15-minute section Total: 75 minutes	Two 25-minute sections One 20-minute section Total: 70 minutes
Content	Arithmetic Algebra I Geometry Data analysis and statistics	Arithmetic Algebra I Algebra II Geometry Data analysis and statistics
Question Types	5-choice multiple-choice Quantitative comparisons Student-produced responses	5-choice multiple-choice Student-produced responses
Score	200–800	200–800

Writing	Current SAT I	New SAT I
Time	N/A	25-minute essay 25-minute multiple-choice section Total: 50 minutes
Content	N/A	Grammar, usage, word choice, and idiom Writing
Question Types	N/A	Essay Multiple-choice section
Score	N/A	800 Essay subscore 2–12

Total	Current SAT I	New SAT I
Time	3 hours (including 30-minute experimental section)	3 hours 35 minutes (including 25-minute experimental section)
Total Perfect Score	1600	2400

So, how does all this affect you? If you are going to graduate from high school and enter college before 2006, you will not be affected by any of these changes. You will take the current exam. If, however, you are going to graduate from high school in 2006 or later, you will take the new exam. There are several ways in which your testing experience will be impacted. The "coveted" perfect SAT score will rise from 1600 to 2400. The new test will be more than half an hour longer than the current test. The additional personnel required to score the essays will result in a higher fee for the exam. Early estimates suggest that the test fee may increase by $10 or $12. And the changes to the content and format of the exam will obviously affect your preparation.

NOTES